Best Stories of O. Henry

Abridged Version

V&S PUBLISHERS

Published by:

V&S PUBLISHERS

F-2/16, Ansari road, Daryaganj, New Delhi-110002
☎ 23240026, 23240027 • *Fax:* 011-23240028
Email: info@vspublishers.com • *Website:* www.vspublishers.com

Regional Office : Hyderabad
5-1-707/1, Brij Bhawan (Beside Central Bank of India Lane)
Bank Street, Koti, Hyderabad - 500 095
☎ 040-24737290
E-mail: vspublishershyd@gmail.com

Branch Office : Mumbai
Jaywant Industrial Estate, 2nd Floor-222, Tardeo Road
Opposite Sobo Central, Mumbai - 400 034
☎ 022-23510736
E-mail: vspublishersmum@gmail.com

Follow us on:

All books available at **www.vspublishers.com**

Printed at: Repro Knowledgecast Ltd., Thane.

Publisher's Note

It has been our constant endeavour at the **V&S Publishers** to publish all kinds of books ranging from Fiction, Non-fiction, Storybooks, Children Encyclopaedias, to Self-Help, Science Books, Dictionaries, Grammar Books, Self-Development, Management Books, etc.

However, this is for the first time that we are venturing into the vast, rich and fathomless ocean of English Literature and have come up with this *storybooks called* authored by O.Henry Abridged Version.There is a lot to learn from his writing style, selection of plot, development and building of theme and suspense of the story, emphasis and presentation of characters, dialogues, working towards the climax of the story, presenting the climax, and then finally concluding the story.

Besides the above mentioned characteristics, the book contains short biography of the author, his brief life history, notable works and literary achievements. Each story has a set of word meanings on each page aiming the school students to help them grasp the essence of the story easily and quickly.

These books are not only a boon for the school-going students, particularly studying in senior classes from the seventh standard till the twelfth, but are also a treasure trove for all those young and aspiring writers, voracious readers and lovers of English language and literature.

Contents

O. Henry

Born on September 11, 1862
Died on June 5, 1910
Pen name: O. Henry, or Oliver Henry
Notable Works: *The Gift of the Magi, The Ransom of Red Chief, The Cop and the Anthem, A Retrieved Reformation, The Duplicity of Hargraves, The Last Leaf,* etc.

Early Life

William Sydney Porter, popularly known by his pen name, **O. Henry**, was born on September 11, 1862 in Greensboro, North Carolina. He was one of the most popular American writers well-known for his short stories, which are full of wit, wordplay, warm characterisation and clever twist endings. His parents were Dr. Algernon Sidney Porter, a physician, and Mary Jane Virginia Swaim Porter. As a child, Porter was always reading, everything from classics to dime novels. Porter graduated from his aunt Evelina Maria Porter's elementary school in 1876. He then enrolled at the Lindsey Street High School. His aunt continued to tutor him until he was fifteen. In 1879, he started working in his uncle's drugstore and in 1881, at the age of nineteen, he was licensed as a pharmacist. At the drugstore, he also showed off his natural artistic talents by sketching the townsfolk.

He then worked full time on his humorous weekly called *The Rolling Stone,* which he started while working at the bank. *The Rolling Stone* featured satire on life, people and politics and included Porter's short stories and sketches. Although eventually, reaching a top circulation of 1500, *The Rolling Stone* failed in April 1895, since the paper never provided an adequate income. However, his writings and drawings had caught the attention of the editor at the Houston Post. Porter and his family moved to Houston in 1895, where he started writing for the *Post.* Porter gathered ideas for his column by loitering in hotel lobbies and observing and talking to people there. This was a technique he used throughout his writing career.

Literary Works and Achievements

Cabbages and Kings was his first collection of stories, followed by *The Four Million.* Among his most famous stories are: *The Gift of the Magi* about a young couple, who are short of money but desperately want to buy each other Christmas gifts; *The Ransom of Red Chief,* in which two men kidnap a boy of ten. The boy turns out to be so bratty and obnoxious that the desperate men ultimately pay the boy's father $250 to take him back, *The Cop and the Anthem, A Retrieved Reformation, The Duplicity of Hargraves, The Last Leaf* and many more.

Writing Style

O. Henry's stories frequently have surprise endings. In his day, he was called the American answer to Guy de Maupassant. Both authors wrote plot twist endings, but O. Henry stories were much more playful. His stories are also known for witty narration. Most of O. Henry's stories are set in his own time, the early 20th century. Many take place in New York City and deal for the most part with ordinary people: clerks, policemen, waitresses, etc.

Later Years

Porter's or O. Henry's most prolific writing period started in 1902, when he moved to New York City to be near his publishers. While there, he wrote about **381 short stories**. He wrote a story a week for over a year for the *New York World Sunday Magazine*. His wit, characterisation, and plot twists were adored by his readers, but often panned by critics.

Porter was a heavy drinker, and his health deteriorated markedly in 1908, which affected his writing. In 1909, his wife, Sarah left him, and he died on June 5, 1910, of cirrhosis of the liver, complications of diabetes, and an enlarged heart. After funeral services in New York City, he was buried in the Riverside Cemetery in Asheville, North Carolina. His daughter, Margaret Worth Porter, who died in 1927, was buried next to her father.

Trivia

The **O. Henry Award** is a prestigious annual prize named after Porter and given to outstanding short stories of the world. Several schools around United States bear Porter's pseudonym.

Past One At Rodney's

ONly on the lower East Side of New York do the houses of Capulet and Montagu survive. There they do not fight by the book of arithmetic. If you but bite your thumb at an upholder of your opposing house you have work cut out for your steel. On Broadway you may drag your man along a dozen blocks by his nose, and he will only bawl for the watch; but in the domain of the East Side Tybalts and Mercutios you must observe the niceties of deportment to the wink of any eyelash and to an inch of elbow room at the bar when its patrons include foes of your house and kin.

So, when Eddie McManus, known to the Capulets as Cork McManus, drifted into Dutch Mike's for a stein of beer, and came upon a bunch of Montagus making merry with the suds, he began to observe the strictest parliamentary rules. Courtesy forbade his leaving the saloon with his thirst unslaked; caution steered him to a place at the bar where the mirror supplied the cognizance of the enemy's movements that his indifferent gaze seemed to disdain; experience whispered to him that the finger of trouble would be busy among the chattering steins at Dutch Mike's that night. Close by his side drew Brick Cleary, his Mercutio, companion of his perambulations. Thus they stood, four of the Mulberry Hill Gang and two for the Dry Dock Gang, minding their P's and Q's so solicitously that Dutch Mike kept one eye on his customers and the other on an open space beneath his bar in which it was his custom to seek safety whenever the ominous politeness of the rival associations congealed into the shapes of bullets and cold steel.

But we have not to do with the wars of the Mulberry Hills and the Dry Docks. We must to Rooney's, where, on the most blighted dead branch of the tree of life, a little pale orchid shall bloom. Overstrained etiquette at last gave way. It is not known who first overstepped the bounds of punctilio; but the consequences were immediate. Buck Malone, of the Mulberry Hills, with a Dewey-like swiftness, got an eight-inch gun swung round from his hurricane deck. But McManus's simile must be the torpedo. He glided in under the guns and slipped a scant three inches of knife blade between the ribs of the

Bawl – *Howl, wail*
Foe – *Enemy*
Courtesy – *Good manners*
Disdain – *Contempt*

Mulberry Hill cruiser. Meanwhile Brick Cleary, a devotee to strategy, had skimmed across the lunch counter and thrown the switch of the electrics, leaving the combat to be waged by the light of gunfire alone. Dutch Mike crawled from his haven and ran into the street crying for the watch instead of for a Shakespeare to immortalize the Cimmerian shindy.

The cop came, and found a prostrate, bleeding Montagu supported by three distrait and reticent followers of the House. Faithful to the ethics of the gangs, no one knew whence the hurt came. There was no Capulet to be seen.

"Raus mit der interrogatories," said Buck Malone to the officer. "Sure I know who done it. I always manage to get a bird's eye view of any guy that comes up an' makes a show case for a hardware store out of me. No. I'm not telling you his name. I'll settle with um meself. Wow - ouch! Easy, boys! Yes, I'll attend to his case meself. I'm not making any complaint."

At midnight McManus strolled around a pile of lumber near an East Side dock, and lingered in the vicinity of a certain water plug. Brick Cleary drifted casually to the trysting place ten minutes later. "He'll maybe not croak," said Brick; "and he won't tell, of course. But Dutch Mike did. He told the police he was tired of having his place shot up. It's unhandy just now, because Tim Corrigan's in Europe for a week's end with Kings. He'll be back on the *Kaiser Williams* next Friday. You'll have to duck out of sight till then. Tim'll fix it up all right for us when he comes back."

This goes to explain why Cork McManus went into Rooney's one night and there looked upon the bright, stranger face of Romance for the first time in his precarious career.

Until Tim Corrigan should return from his jaunt among Kings and Princes and hold up his big white finger in private offices, it was unsafe for Cork in any of the old haunts of his gang. So he lay, perdu, in the high rear room of a Capulet, reading pink sporting sheets and cursing the slow paddle wheels of the *Kaiser Wilhelm*.

It was on Thursday evening that Cork's seclusion became intolerable to him. Never a hart panted for water fountain as he did for the cool touch of a drifting stein, for the firm security of a foot-rail in the hollow of his shoe and the quiet, hearty challenges of friendship, and repartee along and across the shining bars. But he must avoid the district where he was known. The

Ominous – *Threatening, Inauspicious*
Combat – *Battle*
Reticent – *Quiet*
Jaunt – *Outing*
Seclusion – *Privacy*

cops were looking for him everywhere, for news was scarce, and the newspapers were harping again on the failure of the police to suppress the gangs. If they got him before Corrigan came back, the big white finger could not be uplifted; it would be too late then. But Corrigan would be home the next day, so he felt sure there would be small danger in a little excursion that night among the crass pleasures that represented life to him.

At half-past twelve McManus stood in a darkish cross-town street looking up at the name "Rooney's," picked out by incandescent lights against a signboard over a second-story window. He had heard of the place as a tough "hang-out"; with its frequenters and its locality he was unfamiliar. Guided by certain unerring indications common to all such resorts, he ascended the stairs and entered the large room over the cafe.

Here were some twenty or thirty tables, at this time about half-filled with Rooney's guests. Waiters served drinks. At one end a human pianola with drugged eyes hammered the keys with automatic and furious unprecision. At merciful intervals a waiter would roar or squeak a song - songs full of "Mr. Jonsons" and "babes" and "coons" - historical word guaranties of the genuineness of African melodies composed by red waist-coated young gentlemen, natives of the cotton fields, and rice swamps of West Twenty-eighth Street.

For one brief moment you must admire Rooney with me as he receives, seats, manipulates, and chaffs his guests. He is twenty-nine. He has Wellington's nose, Dante's chin, the cheek-bones of an Iroquois, the smile of Talleyrand, Corbett's foot work, and the pose of an eleven-year-old East Side Central Park Queen of the May. He is assisted by a lieutenant known as Frank, a pudgy, easy chap, swell-dressed, who goes among the tables seeing that dull care does not intrude. Now, what is there about Rooney's to inspire all this pother? It is more respectable by daylight; stout ladies with children and mittens and bundles and unpedigreed dogs drop up of afternoons for a stein and a chat. Even by gaslight the diversions are melancholy in the mouth - drink and rag-time, and an occasional surprise when the waiter swabs the suds from under your sticky glass. There is an answer. Transmigration! The soul of Sir Walter Raleigh has traveled from beneath his slashed doublet to a kindred home under Rooney's visible plaid waistcoat. Rooney's is twenty years ahead of the times. Rooney has removed the embargo.

Incandescent –
Glowing
Chaff – *Teasing, Mocking*
intrude – *Break in*
Melancholy – *Sad*

Rooney has spread his cloak upon the soggy crossing of public opinion, and any Elizabeth who treads upon it is as much a queen as another. Attend to the revelation of the secret. In Rooney's ladies may smoke!

McManus sat down at a vacant table. He paid for the glass of beer that he ordered, tilted his narrow-brimmed derby to the back of his brick-dust head, twined his feet among the rungs of his chair, and heaved a sigh of contentment from the breathing spaces of his innermost soul; for this mud honey was clarified sweetness to his taste. The sham gaiety, the hectic glow of counterfeit hospitality, the self-conscious, joyless laughter, the wine-born warmth, the loud music retrieving the hour from frequent whiles of awful and corroding silence, the presence of well-clothed and frank-eyed beneficiaries of Rooney's removal of the restrictions laid upon the weed, the familiar blended odors of soaked lemon peel, flat beer, and *peau d'Espagne* - all these were manna to Cork McManus, hungry for his week in the desert of the Capulet's high rear room.

A girl, alone, entered Rooney's, glanced around with leisurely swiftness, and sat opposite McManus at his table. Her eyes rested upon him for two seconds in the look with which woman reconnoitres all men whom she for the first time confronts. In that space of time she will decide upon one of two things - either to scream for the police, or that she may marry him later on.

Her brief inspection concluded, the girl laid on the table a worn red morocco shopping bag with the inevitable top-gallant sail of frayed lace handkerchief flying from a corner of it. After she had ordered a small beer from the immediate waiter she took from her bag a box of cigarettes and lighted one with slightly exaggerated ease of manner. Then she looked again in the eyes of Cork McManus and smiled.

Instantly the doom of each was sealed.

The unqualified desire of a man to buy clothes and build fires for a woman for a whole lifetime at first sight of her is not uncommon among that humble portion of humanity that does not care for Bradstreet or coats-of-arms or Shaw's plays. Love at first sight has occurred a time or two in high life; but, as a rule, the extempore mania is to be found among unsophisticated creatures such as the dove, the blue-tailed dingbat, and the ten-dollar-a-week clerk. Poets, subscribers to all fiction magazines, and schatchens, take notice.

Revelation
– *Exposure*
Vacant – *Empty*
Mania – *Obsession*
Unsophisticated –
Simple, Naive

Best Stories of O.Henry

With the exchange of the mysterious magnetic current came to each of them the instant desire to lie, pretend, dazzle and deceive, which is the worst thing about the hypocritical disorder known as love.

"Have another beer?" suggested Cork. In his circle the phrase was considered to be a card, accompanied by a letter of introduction and references.

"No, thanks," said the girl, raising her eyebrows and choosing her conventional words carefully. "I - merely dropped in for - a slight refreshment." The cigarette between her fingers seemed to require explanation. "My aunt is a Russian lady," she concluded, "and we often have a post per annual cigarette after dinner at home."

"Cheese it!" said Cork, whom society airs oppressed. "Your fingers are as yellow as mine."

"Say," said the girl, blazing upon him with low-voiced indignation, "what do you think I am? Say, who do you think you are talking to? What?"

She was pretty to look at. Her eyes were big, brown, intrepid, and bright. Under her flat sailor hat, planted jauntily on one side, her crinkly, tawny hair parted and was drawn back, low and massy, in a thick, pendant knot behind. The roundness of girlhood still lingered in her chin and neck, but her cheeks and fingers were thinning slightly.

She looked upon the world with defiance, suspicion, and sullen wonder. Her smart, short tan coat was soiled and expensive. Two inches below her black dress dropped the lowest flounce of a heliotrope silk underskirt. "Beg your pardon," said Cork, looking at her admiringly. "I didn't mean anything. Sure, it's no harm to smoke, Maudy."

"Rooney's," said the girl, softened at once by his amends, "is the only place I know where a lady can smoke. Maybe it ain't a nice habit, but aunty lets us at home. And my name ain't Maudy, if you please; it's Ruby Delamere."

"That's a swell handle," said Cork approvingly. "Mine's McManus - Cor - er - Eddie McManus."

"Oh, you can't help that," laughed Ruby. "Don't apologize."

Cork looked seriously at the big clock on Rooney's wall. The girl's ubiquitous eyes took in the movement.

Oppress – *Dominate*
Indignation – *Anger*
Defiance –
Disobedience
Amends –
Improvement
Ubiquitous –
Omnipresent

"I know it's late," she said, reaching for her bag; "but you know how you want a smoke when you want one. Ain't Rooney's all right? I never saw anything wrong here. This is twice I've been in. I work in a bookbindery on Third Avenue. A lot of us girls have been working overtime three nights a week. They won't let you smoke there, of course.

I just dropped in here on my way home for a puff. Ain't it all right in here? If it ain't, I won't come any more."

"It's a little bit late for you to be out alone anywhere," said Cork. "I'm not wise to this particular joint; but anyhow you don't want to have your picture taken in it for a present to your Sunday School teacher. Have one more beer, and then say I take you home."

"But I don't know you," said the girl, with fine scrupulosity. "I don't accept the company of gentlemen I ain't acquainted with. My aunt never would allow that."

"Why," said Cork McManus, pulling his ear, "I'm the latest thing in suitings with side vents and bell skirt when it comes to escortin' a lady. You bet you'll find me all right, Ruby. And I'll give you a tip as to who I am. My governor is one of the hottest cross-buns of the Wall Street push. Morgan's cab horse casts a shoe every time the old man sticks his head out the window. Me! Well, I'm in trainin' down the Street.

The old man's goin' to put a seat on the Stock Exchange in my stockin' my next birthday. But it all sounds like a lemon to me. What I like is golf and yachtin' and - er - well, say a corkin' fast ten-round bout between welter-weights with walkin' gloves."

"I guess you can walk to the door with me," said the girl hesitatingly, but with a certain pleased flutter. "Still I never heard anything extra good about Wall Street brokers, or sport who go to prize fights, either. Ain't you got any other recommendations?"

"I think you're the swellest looker I've had my lamps on in little old New York," said Cork impressively. "That'll be about enough of that, now. Ain't you the kidder!" She modified her chiding words by a deep, long, beaming, smile-embellished look at her cavalier. "We'll drink our beer before we go, ha?"

Cavalier – *A horseman, Knight*
Suspended – *Postponed*

A waiter sang. The tobacco smoke grew denser, drifting and rising in spirals, waves, tilted layers, cumulus clouds, cataracts and suspended fogs like some fifth element created from the ribs of the ancient four. Laughter and chat grew louder, stimulated by Rooney's liquids and Rooney's gallant hospitality to Lady Nicotine.

One o'clock struck. Downstairs there was a sound of closing and locking doors. Frank pulled down the green shades of the front windows carefully. Rooney went below in the dark hall and stood at the front door, his cigarette cached in the hollow of his hand. Thenceforth whoever might seek admittance must present a countenance familiar to Rooney's hawk's eye - the countenance of a true sport.

Cork McManus and the bookbindery girl conversed absorbedly, with their elbows on the table. Their glasses of beer were pushed to one side, scarcely touched, with the foam on them sunken to a thin white scum. Since the stroke of one the stale pleasures of Rooney's had become renovated and spiced; not by any addition to the list of distractions, but because from that moment the sweets became stolen ones.

The flattest glass of beer acquired the tang of illegality; the mildest claret punch struck a knockout blow at law and order; the harmless and genial company became outlaws, defying authority and rule. For after the stroke of one in such places as Rooney's, where neither bed nor board is to be had, drink may not be set before the thirsty of the city of the four million. It is the law.

"Say," said Cork McManus, almost covering the table with his eloquent chest and elbows, "was that dead straight about you workin' in the bookbindery and livin' at home - and just happenin' in here - and - and all that spiel you gave me?"

"Sure it was," answered the girl with spirit. "Why, what do you think? Do you suppose I'd lie to you? Go down to the shop and ask 'em. I handed it to you on the level."

"On the dead level?" said Cork. "That's the way I want it; because -"

"Because what?"

"I throw up my hands," said Cork. "You've got me goin'. You're the girl I've been lookin' for. Will you keep company with me, Ruby?"

Countenance –
Tolerate
Acquire – *Obtain*
Defy – *Confront*
Eloquent – *Expressive*

"Would you like me to - Eddie?"

"Surest thing. But I wanted a straight story about - about yourself, you know. When a fellow had a girl - a steady girl - she's got to be all right, you know. She's got to be straight goods."

"You'll find I'll be straight goods, Eddie."

"Of course you will. I believe what you told me. But you can't blame me for wantin' to find out. You don't see many girls smokin' cigarettes in places like Rooney's after midnight that are like you."

The girl flushed a little and lowered her eyes. "I see that now," she said meekly. "I didn't know how bad it looked. But I won't do it anymore. And I'll go straight home every night and stay there. And I'll give up cigarettes if you say so, Eddie - I'll cut 'em out from this minute on."

Cork's air became judicial, proprietary, condemnatory, yet sympathetic. "A lady can smoke," he decided, slowly, "at times and places. Why? Because it's bein' a lady that helps her pull it off."

"I'm going to quit. There's nothing to it," said the girl. She flicked the stub of her cigarette to the floor.

"At times and places," repeated Cork. "When I call round for you of evenin's we'll hunt out a dark bench in Stuyvesant Square and have a puff or two. But no more Rooney's at one o'clock - see?"

"Eddie, do you really like me?" The girl searched his hard but frank features eagerly with anxious eyes.

"On the dead level."

"When are you coming to see me - where I live?"

"Thursday - day after tomorrow evenin'. That suit you?"

"Fine. I'll be ready for you. Come about seven. Walk to the door with me tonight and I'll show you where I live. Don't forget, now. And don't you go to see any other girls before then, mister! I bet you will, though."

"On the dead level," said Cork, "you make 'em all look like rag-dolls to me. Honest, you do. I know when I'm suited. On the dead level, I do."

Against the front door down-stairs repeated heavy blows were delivered. The loud crashes resounded in the room above. Only a trip-hammer or a policeman's foot could have

Meek – *Humble*
Condemnatory – *Disapproving*
Anxious – *Nervous*
Assaulted – *A sudden, violent attack*
Panic – *Fright*

been the author of those sounds. Rooney jumped like a bullfrog to a corner of the room, turned off the electric lights and hurried swiftly below. The room was left utterly dark except for the winking red glow of cigars and cigarettes.

A second volley of crashes came up from the assaulted door. A little, rustling, murmuring panic moved among the besieged guests. Frank, cool, smooth, reassuring, could be seen in the rosy glow of the burning tobacco, going from table to table.

"All keep still!" was his caution. "Don't talk or make any noise! Everything will be allright. Now, don't feel the slightest alarm. We'll take care of you all."

Ruby felt across the table until Cork's firm hand closed upon hers. "Are you afraid, Eddie?" she whispered. "Are you afraid you'll get a free ride?"

"Nothin' doin' in the teeth-chatterin' line," said Cork. "I guess Rooney's been slow with his envelope. Don't you worry, girly; I'll look out for you all right."

Yet Mr. McManus's ease was only skin-and-muscle-deep. With the police looking everywhere for Buck Malone's assailant, and with Corrigan still on the ocean wave, he felt that to be caught in a police raid would mean an ended career for him. He wished he had remained in the high rear room of the true Capulet reading the pink extras.

Rooney seemed to have opened the front door below and engaged the police in conference in the dark hall. The wordless low growl of their voices came up the stairway. Frank made a wireless news station of himself at the upper door. Suddenly he closed the door, hurried to the extreme rear of the room and lighted a dim gas jet.

"This way, everybody!" he called sharply. "In a hurry; but no noise, please!"

The guests crowded in confusion to the rear. Rooney's lieutenant swung open a panel in the wall, overlooking the back yard, revealing a ladder already placed for the escape.

"Down and out, everybody!" he commanded. "Ladies first! Less talking, please! Don't crowd! There's no danger."

Assailant – *Attacker*
Fierce – *Violent*
Flee – *Escape*
Descend – *To move/ go down*

Among the last, Cork and Ruby waited their turn at the open panel. Suddenly she swept him aside and clung to his arm fiercely.

"Before we go out," she whispered in his ear - "before anything happens, tell me again, Eddie, do you I - do you really like me?"

"On the dead level," said Cork, holding her close with one arm, "when it comes to you, I'm all in."

When they turned they found they were lost and in darkness. The last of the fleeing customers had descended. Half way across the yard they bore the ladder, stumbling, giggling, hurrying to place it against adjoining low building over the roof of which their only route to safety.

"We may as well sit down," said Cork grimly. "Maybe Rooney will stand the cops off, anyhow."

They sat at a table; and their hands came together again.

A number of men then entered the dark room, feeling their way about. One of them, Rooney himself, found the switch and turned on the electric light. The other man was a cop of the old regime - a big cop, a thick cop, a fuming, abrupt cop - not a pretty cop. He went up to the pair at the table and sneered familiarly at the girl.

"What are you doin' in here?" he asked.

"Dropped in for a smoke," said Cork mildly.

"Had any drinks?"

"Not later than one o'clock."

"Get out - quick!" ordered the cop. Then, "Sit down!" he countermanded.

He took off Cork's hat roughly and scrutinized him shrewdly. "Your name's McManus."

"Bad guess," said Cork. "It's Peterson."

"Cork McManus, or something like that," said the cop. "You put a knife into a man in Dutch Mike's saloon a week ago."

"Aw, forget it!" said Cork, who perceived a shade of doubt in the officer's tones. "You've got my mug mixed with somebody else's."

"Have I? Well, you'll come to the station with me, anyhow, and be looked over. The description fits you all right." The cop twisted his fingers under Cork's collar. "Come on!" he ordered roughly.

Cork glanced at Ruby. She was pale, and her thin nostrils quivered. Her quick eye danced from one man's face

Abrupt – *Sudden*
Countermanded – *Cancelled*
Shrewdly – *Astutely*
Stumble – *To trip or fall while walking/ running*
Fury – *Anger*

to the other as they spoke or moved. What hard luck! Cork was thinking - Corrigan on the briny; and Ruby met and lost almost within an hour! Somebody at the police station would recognize him, without a doubt. Hard luck!

But suddenly the girl sprang up and hurled herself with both arms extended against the cop. His hold on Cork's collar was loosened and he stumbled back two or three paces.

"Don't go so fast, Maguire!" she cried in shrill fury. "Keep your hands off my man! You know me, and you know I'm givin' you good advice. Don't you touch him again! He's not the guy you are lookin' for - I'll stand for that."

"See here, Fanny," said the Cop, red and angry, "I'll take you, too, if you don't look out! How do you know this ain't the man I want? What are you doing in here with him?"

"How do I know?" said the girl, flaming red and white by turns. "Because I've known him a year. He's mine. Oughtn't I to know? And what am I doin' here with him? That's easy."

She stooped low and reached down somewhere into a swirl of flirted draperies, heliotrope and black. An elastic snapped, she threw on the table toward Cork a folded wad of bills. The money slowly straightened itself with little leisurely jerks.

"Take that, Jimmy, and let's go," said the girl. "I'm declarin' the usual dividends, Maguire," she said to the officer. "You had your usual five-dollar graft at the usual corner at ten."

"A lie!" said the cop, turning purple. "You go on my beat again and I'll arrest you every time I see you."

"No, you won't," said the girl. "And I'll tell you why. Witnesses saw me give you the money tonight, and last week, too. I've been getting fixed for you."

Cork put the wad of money carefully into his pocket, and said, "Come on, Fanny; let's have some chop suey before we go home."

"Clear out, quick, both of you, or I'll -"

The cop's bluster trailed away into inconsequentiality.

At the corner of the street the two halted. Cork handed back the money without a word. The girl took it and slipped it slowly into her hand bag.

Her expression was the same she had worn when she entered Rooney's that night - she looked upon the world with defiance, suspicion, and sullen wonder.

Leisurely – *Unhurried*
Halt – *Stop*
Defiance – *Disobedience*
Sullen – *Gloomy*

"I guess I might as well say good-bye here," she said dully. "You won't want to see me again, of course. Will you - shake hands - Mr. McManus."

"I mightn't have got wise if you hadn't give the snap away," said Cork. "Why did you do it?"

"You'd have been pinched if I hadn't. That's why. Ain't that reason enough?" Then she began to cry. "Honest, Eddie, I was goin' to be the best girl in the world.

I hated to be what I am; I hated men; I was ready almost to die when I saw you. And you seemed different from everybody else. And when I found you liked me, too, why, I thought I'd make you believe I was good, and I was goin' to be good.

When you asked to come to my house and see me, why, I'd have died rather than do anything wrong after that. But what's the use of talking about it? I'll say good-bye, if you will, Mr. McManus."

Cork was pulling at his ear. "I knifed Malone," said he. "I was the one the cop wanted."

"Oh, that's all right," said the girl listlessly. "It didn't make any difference about that."

"That was all hot air about Wall Street. I don't do nothin' but hang out with a tough gang on the East Side."

"That was all right, too," repeated the girl. "It didn't make any difference."

Cork straightened himself, and pulled his hat down low. "I could get a job at O'Brien's," he said aloud, but to himself.

"Good-bye," said the girl.

"Come on," said Cork, taking her arm. "I know a place."

Two blocks away he turned with her up the steps of a red brick house facing a little park. "What house is this?" she asked, drawing back. "Why are you going in there?"

A street lamp shone brightly in front. There was a brass nameplate at one side of the closed front doors. Cork drew her firmly up the steps. "Read that," said he.

She looked at the name on the plate, and gave a cry between a moan and a scream. "No, no, no, Eddie! Oh, my God, no! I won't let you do that - not now! Let me go! You shan't

Listless – *Languid*
Moan – *Groan*
Gruffly – *Grumpily*
cunning – *Sly*

do that! You can't - you mus'n't! Not after you know! No, no! Come away quick! Oh, my God! Please, Eddie, come!"

Half fainting, she reeled, and was caught in the bend of his arm. Cork's right hand felt for the electric button and pressed it long.

Another cop - how quickly they scent trouble when trouble is on the wing! - came along, saw them, and ran up the steps. "Here! What are you doing with that girl?" he called gruffly.

"She'll be all right in a minute," said Cork. "It's a straight deal."

"Reverend Jeremiah Jones," read the cop from the doorplate with true detective cunning.

"Correct," said Cork. "On the dead level, we're goin' to get married."

Detective – *A person crime*
Cop – *Police*
Reeled – *To have a sensation of whirling*

🛷 🛷

Food For Thought

"I am going to quit. There's nothing to it." Who said this? What did she want to quit? Do you think that Ruby Delamere was actually a bookbindery girl? Had she fallen dep in love with Eddie McManus?

The Girl And The Graft

THe other day I ran across my old friend Ferguson Pogue. Pogue is a *conscientious* grafter of the highest type. His headquarters is the Western Hemisphere, and his line of business is anything from speculating in town lots on the Great Staked Plains to selling wooden toys in Connecticut, made by *hydraulic pressure* from nutmegs ground to a pulp.

Now and then when Pogue has made a good haul he comes to New York for a rest. He says the jug of wine and loaf of bread and Thou in the wilderness business is about as much rest and pleasure to him as sliding down the bumps at Coney would be to President Taft. "Give me," says Pogue, "a big city for my vacation. Especially New York. I'm not much fond of New Yorkers, and Manhattan is about the only place on the globe where I don't find any."

While in the metropolis Pogue can always be found at one of two places. One is a little second-hand bookshop on Fourth Avenue, where he reads books about his hobbies, Mahometanism and taxidermy. I found him at the other - his hall bedroom in Eighteenth Street - where he sat in his stocking feet trying to pluck "The Banks of the Wabash" out of a small zither. Four years he has practised this tune without arriving near enough to cast the longest trout line to the water's edge. On the dresser lay a blued-steel Colt's forty-five and a tight roll of tens and twenties large enough around to belong to the spring rattlesnake-story class. A chambermaid with a room-cleaning air *fluttered* nearby in the hall, unable to enter or to flee, scandalised by the stocking feet, aghast at the Colt's, yet powerless, with her metropolitan instincts, to remove herself beyond the magic influence of the yellow-hued roll.

I sat on his trunk while Ferguson Pogue talked. No one could be franker or more candid in his conversation. Beside his expression the cry of Henry James for lacteal nourishment at the age of one month would have seemed like a Chaldean cryptogram. He told me stories of his profession with pride, for he considered it an art. And I was curious enough to ask him whether he had known any women who followed it.

Conscientious - *Just, Honest*
Hydraulic pressure - *The dynamic behaviour of fluids*
Fluttered - *Toss about*
Scandalised - *Defamed*

"Ladies?" said Pogue, with Western chivalry. "Well, not to any great extent. They don't amount to much in special lines of graft, because they're all so busy in general lines. What? Why, they have to. Who's got the money in the world? The men. Did you ever know a man to give a woman a dollar without any consideration? A man will shell out his dust to another man free and easy and gratis. But if he drops a penny in one of the machines run by the Madam Eve's Daughters' Amalgamated Association and the pineapple chewing gum don't fall out when he pulls the lever you can hear him kick to the superintendent four blocks away. Man is the hardest proposition a woman has to go up against. He's the low-grade one, and she has to work overtime to make him pay. Two times out of five she's salted. She can't put in *crushers* and costly machinery. He'd notice 'em and be onto the game. They have to pan out what they get, and it hurts their tender hands. Some of 'em are natural *sluice* troughs and can carry out $1,000 to the ton. The dry-eyed ones have to depend on signed letters, false hair, sympathy, the kangaroo walk, cowhide whips, ability to cook, sentimental juries, conversational powers, silk underskirts, ancestry, rouge, anonymous letters, violet sachet powders, witnesses, revolvers, pneumatic forms, carbolic acid, moonlight, cold cream and the evening newspapers."

"You are outrageous, Ferg," I said. "Surely there is none of this 'graft' as you call it, in a perfect and *harmonious* matrimonial union!"

"Well," said Pogue, "nothing that would justify you every time in calling Police Headquarters and ordering out the reserves and a vaudeville manager on a dead run. But it's this way: Suppose you're a Fifth Avenue millionaire, soaring high, on the right side of copper and cappers.

"You come home at night and bring a $9,000,000 diamond brooch to the lady who's staked your for a claim. You hand it over. She says, 'Oh, George!' and looks to see if it's backed. She comes up and kisses you. You've waited for it. You get it. All right. It's graft.

"But I'm telling you about Artemisia Blye. She was from Kansas and she suggested corn in all of its phases. Her hair was as yellow as the silk; her form was as tall and graceful as a stalk in the low grounds during a wet summer; her eyes were as big and startling as bunions, and green was her favorite color.

Crushers - *To press or squeeze with a force that destroys/deforms*
Sluice troughs - *To let out/drain water through a long, narrow, open receptacle*
Harmonious - *Melodious*

"On my last trip into the cool recesses of your *sequestered* city I met a human named Vaucross. He was worth - that is, he had a million. He told me he was in business on the street. 'A sidewalk merchant?' says I, sarcastic. 'Exactly,' says he, 'Senior partner of a paving concern.'

"I kind of took to him. For this reason, I met him on Broadway one night when I was out of heart, luck, tobacco and place. He was all silk hat, diamonds and front. He was all front. If you had gone behind him you would have only looked yourself in the face. I looked like a cross between Count Tolstoy and a June *lobster*. I was out of luck. I had - but let me lay my eyes on that dealer again.

"Vaucross stopped and talked to me a few minutes and then he took me to a high-toned restaurant to eat dinner. There was music, and then some Beethoven, and Bordelaise sauce, and *cussing* in French, and frangipangi, and some hauteur and cigarettes. When I am flush I know them places.

"I declare, I must have looked as bad as a magazine artist sitting there without any money and my hair all rumpled like I was booked to read a chapter from 'Elsie's School Days' at a Brooklyn Bohemian smoker. But Vaucross treated me like a bear hunter's guide. He wasn't afraid of hurting the waiter's feelings.

"'Mr. Pogue,' he explains to me, 'I am using you.'

"'Go on,' says I; 'I hope you don't wake up.'

"And then he tells me, you know, the kind of man he was. He was a New Yorker. His whole ambition was to be noticed. He wanted to be *conspicuous*. He wanted people to point him out and bow to him, and tell others who he was. He said it had been the desire of his life always. He didn't have but a million, so he couldn't attract attention by spending money. He said he tried to get into public notice one time by planting a little public square on the east side with garlic for free use of the poor; but Carnegie heard of it, and covered it over at once with a library in the Gaelic language. Three times he had jumped in the way of automibiles; but the only result was five broken ribs and a notice in the papers that an unknown man, five feet ten, with four amalgam-filled teeth, supposed to be the last of the famous Red Leary gang had been run over.

"'Ever try the reporters,' I asked him.

Sequestered - *Te remove/withdraw into solitude*
Lobster - *A large sized prawn*
Cussing - *Swearing, curseny*
Conspicuous - *Clearly, vividly*

"'Last month,' says Mr. Vaucross, 'my expenditure for lunches to reporters was $124.80.'

"'Get anything out of that?' I asks.

"'That reminds me,' says he; 'add $8.50 for perpsin. Yes, I got indigestion.'

"'How am I supposed to push along your scramble for prominence?' I inquires. 'Contrast?'

"'Something of that sort to-night,' says Vaucross. 'It grieves me; but I am forced to resort to *eccentricity*.' And here he drops his napkin in his soup and rises up and bows to a gent who is devastating a potato under a palm across the room.

"'The Police Commissioner,' says my climber, gratified. 'Friend', says I, in a hurry, 'have ambitions but don't kick a rung out of your ladder. When you use me as a stepping stone to salute the police you spoil my appetite on the grounds that I may be degraded and *incriminated*. Be thoughtful.'

"At the Quaker City squab en casserole the idea about Artemisia Blye comes to me.

"'Suppose I can manage to get you in the papers,' says I - 'a column or two every day in all of 'em and your picture in most of 'em for a week. How much would it be worth to you?' "'Ten thousand dollars,' says Vaucross, warm in a minute. 'But no murder,' says he; 'and I won't wear pink pants at a cotillon.'

"'I wouldn't ask you to,' says I. 'This is honourable, stylish and uneffiminate. Tell the waiter to bring a demi tasse and some other beans, and I will disclose to you the opus moderandi.' "We closed the deal an hour later in the rococo rouge et noise room. I telegraphed that night to Miss Artemisia in Salina. She took a couple of photographs and an autograph letter to an elder in the Fourth Presbyterian Church in the morning, and got some transportation and $80. She stopped in Topeka long enough to trade a flashlight interior and a valentine to the vice-president of a trust company for a mileage book and a package of five-dollar notes with $250 scrawled on the band.

"The fifth evening after she got my wire she was waiting, all decolletee and dressed up, for me and Vaucross to take her to dinner in one of these New York feminine apartment houses where a man can't get in unless he plays *bezique* and

Bezique - *A card game*
Incriminated - *Accused*
Eccentricity - *Madness, Craziness*

smokes depilatory powder cigarettes. "'She's a stunner,' says Vaucross when he saw her. 'They'll give her a two-column cut sure.' "This was the scheme the three of us concocted. It was business straight through. Vaucross was to rush Miss Blye with all the style and display and emotion he could for a month. Of course, that amounted to nothing as far as his ambitions were concerned. The sight of a man in a white tie and patent leather pumps pouring greenbacks through the large end of a *cornucopia* to purchase nutriment and heartsease for tall, *willowy blondes* in New York is as common a sight as blue turtles in delirium tremens. But he was to write her love letters - the worst kind of love letters, such as your wife publishes after you are dead - every day. At the end of the month he was to drop her, and she would bring suit for $100,000 for breach of promise.

"Miss Artemisia was to get $10,000. If she won the suit that was all; and if she lost she was to get it anyhow. There was a signed contract to that effect.

"Sometimes they had me out with 'em, but not often. I couldn't keep up to their style. She used to pull out his notes and criticize them like bills of lading.

"'Say, you!' she'd say. 'What do you call this - letter to a Hardware Merchant from His Nephew on Learning that His Aunt Has Nettlerash? You Eastern *duffers* know as much about writing love letters as a Kansas grasshopper does about *tugboats*. "My dear Miss Blye!" - wouldn't that put pink icing and a little red sugar bird on your bridal cake? How long do you expect to hold an audience in a court-room with that kind of stuff? You want to get down to business, and call me "Tweedlums Babe" and "Honeysuckle," and sing yourself "Mama's Own Big Bad Puggy Wuggy Boy" if you want any limelight to concentrate upon your *sparse* gray hairs. Get *sappy*.'

"After that Vaucross dipped his pen in the indelible tabasco. His notes read like something or other in the original. I could see a jury sitting up, and women tearing one another's hats to hear 'em read. And I could see piling up for Mr. Vaucross as much *notoriousness* as Archbishop Crammer or the Brooklyn Bridge or cheese-on-salad ever enjoyed. He seemed mighty pleased at the prospects.

"They agreed on a night; and I stood on Fifth Avenue outside a solemn restaurant and watched 'em. A process-server

Cornucoupla - A horn containing atundant supply food, drink
Willowy - Slender, graceful
Blodes - Having fair hair and vsually fair skin and light eyes
Duffers - Plading, clumy person
Tugboats - Small, Powerful boats

walked in and handed Vaucross the papers at this table. Everybody looked at 'em; and he looked as proud as Cicero. I went back to my room and lit a five-cent cigar, for I knew the $10,000 was as good as ours.

"About two hours later somebody knocked at my door. There stood Vaucross and Miss Artemisia, and she was clinging - yes, sir, clinging - to his arm. And they tells me they'd been out and got married. And they *articulated* some trivial *cadences* about love and such. And they laid down a bundle on the table and said 'Good night' and left.

"And that's why I say," concluded Ferguson Pogue, "that a woman is too busy occupied with her natural vocation and instinct of graft such as is given her for self-preservation and amusement to make any great success in special lines."

"What was in the bundle they left?" I asked, with my usual curiosity.

"Why," said Ferguson, "there was a scalper's railroad ticket as far as Kansas City and two pairs of Mr. Vaucross's old pants."

Food For Thought

Why do you think Miss Artemisia choose Vaucross as her husband instead of Ferguson Pogue? Explain your answer with appropriate reasons.

Articulated - *Made clear or distinct*
Caences - *Arhythmic pattern of sounds/ beats*
Amusement - *Recreation, enjoyment*

The Robe Of Peace

MYsteries follow one another so closely in a great city that the reading public and the friends of Johnny Bellchambers have ceased to marvel at his sudden and unexplained disappearance nearly a year ago. This particular mystery has now been cleared up, but the solution is so strange and *incredible* to the mind of the average man that only a select few who were in close touch with Bellchambers will give it full *credence*.

Johnny Bellchambers, as is well known, belonged to the intrinsically inner circle of the *elite*. Without any of the ostentation of the fashionable ones who endeavor to attract notice by eccentric display of wealth and show he still was *au fait* in everything that gave deserved *lustre* to his high position in the ranks of society.

Especially did he shine in the matter of dress. In this he was the despair of *imitators*. Always correct, *exquisitely* groomed, and possessed of an unlimited wardrobe, he was conceded to be the best-dressed man in New York, and, therefore, in America. There was not a tailor in Gotham who would not have deemed it a precious boon to have been granted the privilege of making Bellchambers' clothes without a cent of pay. As he wore them, they would have been a priceless advertisement.

Trousers were his special passion. Here nothing but perfection would he notice. He would have worn a patch as quickly as he would have overlooked a wrinkle. He kept a man in his apartments always busy pressing his *ample* supply. His friends said that three hours was the limit of time that he would wear these garments without exchanging.

Bellchambers disappeared very suddenly. For three days his absence brought no alarm to his friends, and then they began to operate the usual methods of inquiry. All of them failed. He had left absolutely no trace behind. Then the search

Incredible - *Extraordinary*
Credence - *Acceptance or belief*
Elite - *Person of the highest class*
Lustre - *Sheen*
Imitators - *Copy, follow*
Exquisitely - *Of special beauty/charm*
Ample - *Enough*

for a motive was instituted, but none was found. He had no enemies, he had no debts, there was no woman.

There were several thousand dollars in his bank to his credit. He had never showed any tendency toward mental eccentricity; in fact, he was of a particularly calm and well-balanced *temperament*. Every means of tracing the vanished man was made use of, but without avail. It was one of those cases - more numerous in late years - where men seem to have gone out like the flame of a candle, leaving not even a trail of smoke as a witness.

In May, Tom Eyres and Lancelot Gilliam, two of Bellchambers' old friends, went for a little run on the other side. While *pottering* around in Italy and Switzerland, they happened, one day, to hear of a monastery in the Swiss Alps that promised something outside of the ordinary tourist-*beguiling* attractions. The monastery was almost inaccessible to the average sightseer, being on an extremely rugged and precipitous spur of the mountains. The attractions it possessed but did not advertise were, first, an exclusive and divine *cordial* made by the monks that was said to far surpass benedictine and chartreuse.

Next a huge brass bell so purely and accurately cast that it had not ceased sounding since it was first rung three hundred years ago. Finally, it was asserted that no Englishman had ever set foot within its walls. Eyres and Gilliam decided that these three reports called for investigation.

It took them two days with the aid of two guides to reach the monastery of St. Gondrau. It stood upon a frozen, wind-swept crag with the snow piled about it in treacherous, drifting masses. They were hospitably received by the brothers whose duty it was to entertain the infrequent guest. They drank of the precious cordial, finding it rarely potent and reviving. They listened to the great, ever-echoing bell, and learned that they were pioneer travelers, in those gray stone walls, over the Englishman whose restless feet have trodden nearly every corner of the earth.

At three o'clock on the afternoon they arrived, the two young Gothamites stood with good Brother Cristofer in the

Pacing - *The rate of movement*
Treading - *Walking or Trampling*
Temperament - *Attitude/Nature*
Pottering - *Making pottery*
Beguiling - *To influence by trickery/ flattery*

great, cold hallway of the monastery to watch the monks march past on their way to the refectory. They came slowly, *pacing* by twos, with their heads bowed, *treading* noiselessly with sandaled feet upon the rough stone flags. As the procession slowly filed past, Eyres suddenly gripped Gilliam by the arm. "Look," he whispered, eagerly, "at the one just opposite you now - the one on this side, with his hand at his waist - if that isn't Johnny Bellchambers then I never saw him!"

Gilliam saw and *recognized* the lost glass of fashion.

"What the *deuce*," said he, wonderingly, "is old Bell doing here? Tommy, it surely can't be he! Never heard of Bell having a turn for the religious. Fact is, I've heard him say things when a four-in-hand didn't seem to tie up just right that would bring him up for *court-martial* before any church."

"It's Bell, without a doubt," said Eyres, firmly, "or I'm pretty badly in need of an oculist. But think of Johnny Bellchambers, the Royal High Chancellor of swell togs and the Mahatma of pink teas, up here in cold storage doing penance in a snuff-coloured bathrobe! I can't get it straight in my mind. Let's ask the jolly old boy that's doing honours."

Brother Cristofer was appealed to for information. By that time the monks had passed into the refectory. He could not tell to which one they referred. Bellchambers? Ah, the brothers of St. Gondrau abandoned their worldly names when they took the vows. Did the gentlemen wish to speak with one of the brothers? If they would come to the refectory and indicate the one they wished to see, the reverend abbot in authority would, doubtless, permit it.

Eyres and Gilliam went into the dining hall and pointed out to Brother Cristofer the man they had seen. Yes, it was Johnny Bellchambers. They saw his face plainly now, as he sat among the *dingy* brothers, never looking up, eating broth from a coarse, brown bowl. Permission to speak to one of the brothers was granted to the two travellers by the *abbot*, and they waited in a reception room for him to come. When he did come, treading softly in his sandals, both Eyres and Gilliam looked at him in perplexity and astonishment. It was Johnny Bellchambers, but he had a different look.

Rapturous - *Experiencing great joy/delight*
Ineffable - *In capable of being, described in words*
Dingy - *Shabby*
Deuce - *A cost or point of two*
Abbot - *The superior of an abbey of monks*

Upon his smooth-shaven face was an expression of *ineffable* peace, of *rapturous* attainment, of perfect and complete happiness. His form was proudly erect, his eyes shone with a *serene* and gracious light. He was as neat and well-groomed as in the old New York days, but how differently was he clad! Now he seemed clothed in but a single garment - a long robe of rough brown cloth, gathered by a cord at the waist, and falling in straight, loose folds nearly to his feet. He shook hands with his visitors with his old ease and grace of manner. If there was any embarrassment in that meeting it was not manifested by Johnny Bellchambers. The room had no seats; they stood to converse.

"Glad to see you, old man," said Eyres, somewhat awkwardly. "Wasn't expecting to find you up here. Not a bad idea though, after all. Society's an awful sham. Must be a relief to shake the giddy whirl and retire to - er - *contemplation* and - er - prayer and hymns, and those things.

"Oh, cut that, Tommy," said Bellchambers, cheerfully. "Don't be afraid that I'll pass around the plate. I go through these thing-um-bobs with the rest of these old boys because they are the rules. I'm Brother Ambrose here, you know. I'm given just ten minutes to talk to you fellows. That's rather a new design in waistcoats you have on, isn't it, Gilliam? Are they wearing those things on Broadway now?"

"It's the same old Johnny," said Gilliam, joyfully. "What the devil - I mean why - Oh, confound it! what did you do it for, old man?"

"Peel the bathrobe," pleaded Eyres, almost tearfully, "and go back with us. The old crowd'll go wild to see you. This isn't in your line, Bell. I know half a dozen girls that wore the willow on the quiet when you shook us in that unaccountable way. Hand in your resignation, or get a *dispensation*, or whatever you have to do to get a release from this ice factory. You'll get catarrh here, Johnny - and - My God! you haven't any socks on!"

Contemplation - *Deep consideration, reflection, intention*
Dispensation - *Distribution*
Caressinghy - *An act/gresture expressing offection*
Reverberated - *Rebounded, recoiled*

Bellchambers looked down at his sandaled feet and smiled.

"You fellows don't understand," he said, **soothingly**. "It's nice of you to want me to go back, but the old life will never know me again. I have reached here the goal of all my ambitions.

I am entirely happy and contented. Here I shall remain for the remainder of my days. You see this robe that I wear?" Bellchambers **caressingly** touched the straight-hanging garment: "At last I have found something that will not bag at the knees. I have attained -"

At that moment the deep boom of the great brass bell **reverberated** through the monastery. It must have been a **summons** to immediate devotions, for Brother Ambrose bowed his head, turned and left the chamber without another word. A slight wave of his hand as he passed through the stone doorway seemed to say a farewell to his old friends. They left the monastery without seeing him again.

And this is the story that Tommy Eyres and Lancelot Gilliam brought back with them from their latest European tour.

Food For Thought

What do you think Johnny Bellchambers was doing in the monastery? Why did he become a monk and said to his friends, "You see this robe that I wear?" At last, I have found something that will not bag at the knees. I have reached here – the goal of all my ambitions." Think deeply, before giving an appropriate answer.

Mirth - *Amusement, laughter*
Partaken - *Receive, take or have a part*
Resentment - *The feeling of displeasure*
Smoldered - *To burn without flame*
Friendly - *Agreeable*

Best Stories of O.Henry

Proof Of The Pudding

SPring winked a vitreous optic at Editor Westbrook of the *Minerva Magazine*, and deflected him from his course. He had lunched in his favourite corner of a Broadway hotel, and was returning to his office when his feet became entangled in the lure of the vernal *coquette*. Which is by way of saying that he turned eastward in Twenty-sixth Street, safely forded the spring freshet of vehicles in Fifth Avenue, and meandered along the walks of budding Madison Square.

The lenient air and the settings of the little park almost formed a pastoral; the color *motif* was green - the presiding shade at the creation of man and vegetation.

The callow grass between the walks was the colour of verdigris, a poisonous green, *reminiscent* of the horde of derelict humans that had breathed upon the soil during the summer and autumn. The bursting tree buds looked strangely familiar to those who had botanised among the *garnishings* of the fish course of a forty-cent dinner. The sky above was of that pale aquamarine tint that ballroom poets rhyme with "true" and "Sue" and "coo." The one natural and frank color visible was the ostensible green of the newly painted benches - a shade between the color of a pickled cucumber and that of a last year's fast-black *cravenette* raincoat. But, to the city-bred eye of Editor Westbrook, the landscape appeared a masterpiece.

And now, whether you are of those who rush in, or of the gentle *concourse* that fears to tread, you must follow in a brief invasion of the editor's mind.

Editor Westbrook's spirit was contented and serene. The April number of the *Minerva* had sold its entire edition before the tenth day of the month - a newsdealer in Keokuk had written that he could have sold fifty copies more if he had 'em. The owners of the magazine had raised his (the editor's) salary; he had just installed in his home a jewel of a recently imported cook who was afraid of policemen; and the morning papers had published in full a speech he had made at a publishers' banquet. Also there were echoing in his mind the jubilant notes of a splendid song that his charming young wife had sung to him before he left his up-town apartment that morning. She

Coquette - *A woman who flirts lighthearted with man*
Motif - *A dominant idea feature*
Reminiscent - *Stimulating memories*
Cravenetle - *Timidly*
Concourse - *Assemblase*

was taking *enthusiastic* interest in her music of late, practising early and diligently. When he had complimented her on the improvement in her voice she had fairly hugged him for joy at his praise. He felt, too, the benign, tonic medicament of the trained nurse, Spring, tripping softly adown the wards of the *convalescent* city.

While Editor Westbrook was sauntering between the rows of park benches (already filling with vagrants and the guardians of lawless childhood) he felt his sleeve grasped and held. Suspecting that he was about to be *panhandled,* he turned a cold and unprofitable face, and saw that his captor was - Dawe - Shackleford Dawe, dingy, almost ragged, the *genteel* scracely visible in him through the deeper lines of the shabby.

While the editor is pulling himself out of his surprise, a flashlight biography of Dawe is offered.

He was a fiction writer, and one of Westbrook's old acquaintances. At one time they might have called each other old friends. Dawe had some money in those days, and lived in a decent apartment house near Westbrook's. The two families often went to theatres and dinners together. Mrs. Dawe and Mrs. Westbrook became "dearest" friends. Then one day a little tentacle of the octopus, just to amuse itself, ingurgitated Dawe's capital, and he moved to the Gramercy Park neighborhood where one, for a few groats per week, may sit upon one's trunk under eight-branched chandeliers and opposite Carrara marble **mantels** and watch the mice play upon the floor. Dawe thought to live by writing fiction. Now and then he sold a story. He submitted many to Westbrook.

The *Minerva* printed one or two of them; the rest were returned. Westbrook sent a careful and conscientious personal letter with each rejected manuscript, pointing out in detail his reasons for considering it unavailable. Editor Westbrook had his own clear conception of what constituted good fiction. So had Dawe. Mrs. Dawe was mainly concerned about the constituents of the scanty dishes of food that she managed to scrape together.

One day Dawe had been spouting to her about the *excellencies* of certain French writers. At dinner they sat down to a dish that a hungry schoolboy could have *encompassed* at a gulp. Dawe commented.

Convalescent - *Gradual return to health after illness*
Genteelc - *Well-bred, refined*
Mantels - *Wooden/ stone frame around the opening of a fireplace*

"It's Maupassant hash," said Mrs. Dawe. "It may not be art, but I do wish you would do a five-course Marion Crawford serial with an Ella Wheeler Wilcox *sonnet* for dessert. I'm hungry."

As far as this from success was Shackleford Dawe when he plucked Editor Westbrook's sleeve in Madison Square. That was the first time the editor had seen Dawe in several months.

"Why, Shack, is this you?" said Westbrook, somewhat awkwardly, for the form of his phrase seemed to touch upon the other's changed appearance.

"Sit down for a minute," said Dawe, *tugging* at his sleeve. "This is my office. I can't come to yours, looking as I do. Oh, sit down - you won't be disgraced. Those half-plucked birds on the other benches will take you for a swell porch-climber. They won't know you are only an editor."

"Smoke, Shack?" said Editor Westbrook, sinking cautiously upon the *virulent* green bench. He always yielded gracefully when he did yield.

Dawe snapped at the cigar as a kingfisher darts at a sunperch, or a girl pecks at a chocolate cream.

"I have just -" began the editor.

"Oh, I know; don't finish," said Dawe. "Give me a match. You have just ten minutes to spare. How did you manage to get past my office-boy and invade my sanctum? There he goes now, throwing his club at a dog that couldn't read the 'Keep off the Grass' signs."

"How goes the writing?" asked the editor.

"Look at me," said Dawe, "for your answer. Now don't put on that embarrassed, friendly-but-honest look and ask me why I don't get a job as a wine agent or a cab driver. I'm in the fight to a finish. I know I can write good fiction and I'll force you fellows to admit it yet. I'll make you change the spelling of 'regrets' to 'c-h-e-q-u-e' before I'm done with you."

Editor Westbrook gazed through his nose-glasses with a sweetly sorrowful, omniscient, sympathetic, skeptical expression - the copyrighted expression of the editor *beleagured* by the unavailable contributor.

"Have you read the last story I sent you - 'The Alarum of the Soul'?" asked Dawe.

Sonnet - *A poem of 14 lines*
Tugging - *To pull at*
Virulent - *Actively, poisonous*
Beleagred - *With forces*

"Carefully. I hesitated over that story, Shack, really I did. It had some good points. I was writing you a letter to send with it when it goes back to you. I regret -"

"Never mind the regrets," said Dawe, grimly. "There's neither salve nor sting in 'em any more. What I want to know is *why*. Come now; out with the good points first."

"The story," said Westbrook, *deliberately*, after a suppressed sigh, "is written around an almost original plot. Characterisation - the best you have done. Construction - almost as good, except for a few weak joints which might be strengthened by a few changes and touches. It was a good story, except -"

"I can write English, can't I?" interrupted Dawe.

"I have always told you," said the editor, "that you had a style."

"Then the trouble is -"

"Same old thing," said Editor Westbrook. "You work up to your climax like an artist. And then you turn yourself into a photographer. I don't know what form of obstinate madness possesses you, but that is what you do with everything that you write.

No, I will retract the comparison with the photographer. Now and then photography, in spite of its impossible perspective, manages to record a fleeting glimpse of truth. But you spoil every *denouement* by those flat, drab, obliterating strokes of your brush that I have so often complained of. If you would rise to the literary pinnacle of your dramatic senses, and paint them in the high colors that art requires, the postman would leave fewer bulky, self-addressed envelopes at your door."

"Oh, *fiddles* and footlights!" cried Dawe, derisively. "You've got that old sawmill drama kink in your brain yet. When the man with the black mustache kidnaps golden-haired Bessie you are bound to have the mother kneel and raise her hands in the spotlight and say: 'May high heaven witness that I will rest neither night nor day till the heartless villain that has stolen me child feels the weight of another's vengeance!'"

Editor Westbrook conceded a smile of *impervious complacency.*

"I think," said he, "that in real life the woman would express herself in those words or in very similar ones."

"Not in a six hundred nights' run anywhere but on the stage," said Dawe hotly. "I'll tell you what she'd say in real life. She'd say: 'What! Bessie led away by a strange man? Good Lord! It's one trouble after another! Get my other hat, I must hurry around to the police-station. Why wasn't somebody looking after her, I'd like to know?

For God's sake, get out of my way or I'll never get ready. Not that hat - the brown one with the velvet bows. Bessie must have been crazy; she's usually shy of strangers. Is that too much powder? Lordy! How I'm upset!'

"That's the way she'd talk," continued Dawe. "People in real life don't fly into heroics and blank verse at emotional crises. They simply can't do it. If they talk at all on such occasions they draw from the same vocabulary that they use every day, and muddle up their words and ideas a little more, that's all."

"Shack," said Editor Westbrook impressively, "did you ever pick up the *mangled* and lifeless form of a child from under the *fender* of a street car, and carry it in your arms and lay it down before the *distracted* mother? Did you ever do that and listen to the words of grief and despair as they flowed spontaneously from her lips?"

"I never did," said Dawe. "Did you?"

"Well, no," said Editor Westbrook, with a slight frown. "But I can well imagine what she would say."

"So can I," said Dawe.

And now the fitting time had come for Editor Westbrook to play the oracle and silence his opinionated contributor. It was not for an unarrived fictionist to dictate words to be uttered by the heroes and heroines of the *Minerva Magazine*, contrary to the theories of the editor thereof.

"My dear Shack," said he, "if I know anything of life I know that every sudden, deep and tragic emotion in the human heart calls forth an apposite, concordant, conformable and proportionate expression of feeling.

How much of this inevitable accord between expression and feeling should be attributed to nature, and how much to the influence of art, it would be difficult to say. The *sublimely* terrible roar of the lioness that has been deprived of her cubs is

Mangled - *Severely, disfigure*
Fender - *A device on the front of a locomotive*
Sublimely - *Completely, absolutely*
Histrionic - *Overly dramatic*

dramatically as far above her customary whine and purr as the kingly and transcendent utterances of Lear are above the level of his senile vaporings. But it is also true that all men and women have what may be called a sub-conscious dramatic sense that is awakened by a sufficiently deep and powerful emotion - a sense unconsciously acquired from literature and the stage that prompts them to express those emotions in language *befitting* their importance and *histrionic* value."

"And in the name of the seven sacred saddle-blankets of Sagittarius, where did the stage and literature get the stunt?" asked Dawe.

"From life," answered the editor, triumphantly.

The story writer rose from the bench and *gesticulated eloquently* but dumbly. He was beggared for words with which to formulate adequately his dissent.

On a bench nearby a frowzy loafer opened his red eyes and *perceived* that his moral support was due a downtrodden brother.

"Punch him one, Jack," he called hoarsely to Dawe. "W'at's he come makin' a noise like a penny arcade for amongst gen'lemen that comes in the square to set and think?"

Editor Westbrook looked at his watch with an affected show of leisure.

"Tell me," asked Dawe, with *truculent* anxiety, "what especial faults in 'The Alarum of the Soul' caused you to throw it down?"

"When Gabriel Murray," said Westbrook, "goes to his telephone and is told that his fiancee has been shot by a burglar, he says - I do not recall the exact words, but -"

"I do," said Dawe. "He says: 'Damn Central; she always cuts me off.' (And then to his friend) 'Say, Tommy, does a thirty-two bullet make a big hole? It's kind of hard luck, ain't it? Could you get me a drink from the sideboard, Tommy? No; straight; nothing on the side.'"

"And again," continued the editor, without pausing for argument, "when Berenice opens the letter from her husband informing her that he has fled with the manicure girl, her words are - let me see -"

"She says," *interposed* the author: "'Well, what do you think of that!'"

Gesticulated - *To express in gestures*
Eloquently - *Fluently*
Truculent - *Firece, cruel*
Colloquialisms - *Informal words*
Doggedly - *Stubbornly*

"Absurdly inappropriate words," said Westbrook, "presenting an anti-climax - plunging the story into hopeless bathos. Worse yet; they mirror life falsely. No human being ever uttered banal *colloquialisms* when *confronted* by sudden tragedy."

"Wrong," said Dawe, closing his unshaven jaws **doggedly**. "I say no man or woman ever spouts 'high-falutin' talk when they go up against a real climax. They talk naturally and a little worse."

The editor rose from the bench with his air of *indulgence* and inside information.

"Say, Westbrook," said Dawe, *pinning* him by the *lapel*, "would you have accepted 'The Alarum of the Soul' if you had believed that the actions and words of the characters were true to life in the parts of the story that we discussed?"

"It is very likely that I would, if I believed that way," said the editor. "But I have explained to you that I do not."

"If I could prove to you that I am right?"

"I'm sorry, Shack, but I'm afraid I haven't time to argue any further just now."

"I don't want to argue," said Dave. "I want to demonstrate to you from life itself that my view is the correct one."

"How could you do that?" asked Westbrook, in a surprised tone.

"Listen," said the writer, seriously. "I have thought of a way. It is important to me that my theory of true-to-life fiction be recognised as correct by the magazines. I've fought for it for three years, and I'm down to my last dollar, with two months' rent due."

"I have applied the opposite of your theory," said the editor, "in selecting the fiction for the *Minerva Magazine*. The circulation has gone up from ninety thousand to -"

"Four hundred thousand," said Dawe. "Whereas it should have been **boosted** to a million."

"You said something to me just now about demonstrating your pet theory."

"I will. If you'll give me about half an hour of your time I'll prove to you that I am right. I'll prove it by Louise."

"Your wife!" exclaimed Westbrook. "How?"

"Well, not exactly by her, but *with* her," said Dawe. "Now, you know how devoted and loving Louse has always been.

Indulgence -
Tolerance
Pinning -*Longing*
Lapel - *Especially*
a continuation of at
collar
Boosted - *Lifted/*
Raised

She thinks I'm the only genuine preparation on the market that bears the old doctor's signature. She's been fonder and more faithful than ever, since I've been cast for the neglected genius part."

"Indeed, she is a charming and admirable life companion," agreed the editor. "I remember what inseparable friends she and Mrs. Westbrook once were. We are both lucky chaps, Shack, to have such wives. You must bring Mrs. Dawe up some evening soon, and we'll have one of those informal chafing-dish suppers that we used to enjoy so much."

"Later," said Dawe. "When I get another shirt. And now I'll tell you my scheme. When I was about to leave home after breakfast - if you can call tea and oatmeal breakfast - Louise told me she was going to visit her aunt in Eighty-ninth Street. She said she would return at three o'clock. She is always on time to a minute. It is now -"

Dawe glanced toward the editor's watch pocket.

"Twenty-seven minutes to three," said Westbrook, scanning his time-piece.

"We have just enough time," said Dawe. "We will go to my flat at once. I will write a note, address it to her and leave it on the table where she will see it as she enters the door. You and I will be in the dining-room concealed by the *portieres*. In that note I'll say that I have fled from her forever with an affinity who understands the need of my artistic soul as she never did. When she reads it we will observe her actions and hear her words. Then we will know which theory is the correct one - yours or mine."

"Oh, never!" exclaimed the editor, shaking his head. "That would be *inexcusably* cruel. I could not consent to have Mrs. Dawe's feelings played upon in such a manner."

"Brace up," said the writer. "I guess I think as much of her as you do. It's for her benefit as well as mine. I've got to get a market for my stories in some way.

It won't hurt Louise. She's healthy and sound. Her heart goes as strong as a ninety-eight-cent watch. It'll last for only a minute, and then I'll step out and explain to her. You really owe it to me to give me the chance, Westbrook."

Editor Westbrook at length yielded, though but half willingly. And in the half of him that consented lurked the *vivisectionist* that is in all of us. Let him who has not used

Portieres - *Curtains hung in a doorway*
Inexcusably - *Incapable of being excused/justified*
Vivisectionist - *A person who dissects the living body*

Best Stories of O.Henry

the scalpel rise and stand in his place. Pity 'tis that there are not enough rabbits and guinea-pigs to go around.

The two experimenters in Art left the Square and hurried eastward and then to that south until they arrived in the Gramercy neighbourhood.

Within its high iron railings the little park had put on its smart coat of *vernal* green, and was admiring itself in its fountain mirror. Outside the railings the hollow square of crumbling houses, shells of a *bygone* gentry, leaned as if in ghostly gossip over the forgotten doings of the vanished quality. *Sic transit gloria urbis.*

A block or two north of the Park, Dawe steered the editor again eastward, then, after covering a short distance, into a lofty but narrow flathouse burdened with a *floridly* over-decorated *fa,cade.* To the fifth story they toiled, and Dawe, panting, pushed his latch-key into the door of one of the front flats.

When the door opened Editor Westbrook saw, with feelings of pity, how meanly and *meagerly* the rooms were furnished.

"Get a chair, if you can find one," said Dawe, "while I hunt up pen and ink. Hello, what's this? Here's a note from Louise. She must have left it there when she went out this morning."

He picked up an envelope that lay on the centre-table and tore it open. He began to read the letter that he drew out of it; and once having begun it aloud he so read it through to the end. These are the words that Editor Westbrook heard:

"Dear Shackleford:

"By the time you get this I will be about a hundred miles away and still a-going. I've got a place in the chorus of the Occidental Opera Co., and we start on the road to-day at twelve o'clock. I didn't want to starve to death, and so I decided to make my own living. I'm not coming back. Mrs. Westbrook is going with me.

She said she was tired of living with a combination *phonograph*, iceberg and dictionary, and she's not coming back, either. We've been practising the songs and dances for two months on the quiet. I hope you will be successful, and get along all right! Good-bye.

Floridly - *Reddish, ruddy*
Meagerly - *Hardly*
Phonograph - *A form of gramophone*
Blurted - *Revealed, utter suddenly*

"Louise."

Dawe dropped the letter, covered his face with his trembling hands, and cried out in a deep, vibrating voice:

"My God, why hast thou given me this cup to drink? Since she is false, then let Thy Heaven's fairest gifts, faith and love, become the jesting by-words of traitors and fiends!"

Editor Westbrook's glasses fell to the floor. The fingers of one hand **fumbled** with a button on his coat as he **blurted** between his pale lips:

"Say, Shack, ain't that a hell of a note? Wouldn't that knock you off your perch, Shack? Ain't it hell, now, Shack - ain't it?"

Food For Thought

O.Henry is known for surprise endings. Dawe was an unsuccessful writer and Westbrook, a struggling editor of a magazine, who had recently got a salary raise. Both their wives, particularly, Dawe's wife, Louise was totally disappointed by her husband's unsuccessful career. Do you like the ending of the stroy? Answer in Yes, or No and give reasons for your answer.

Babes In The Jungle

MOntague Silver, the finest street man and art grafter in the West, says to me once in Little Rock: "If you ever lose your mind, Billy, and get too old to do honest *swindling* among grown men, go to New York. In the West a sucker is born every minute; but in New York they appear in chunks of roe - you can't count 'em!"

Two years afterward I found that I couldn't remember the names of the Russian admirals, and I noticed some gray hairs over my left ear; so I knew the time had arrived for me to take Silver's advice.

I struck New York about noon one day, and took a walk up Broadway. And I run against Silver himself, all encompassed up in a spacious kind of haberdashery, leaning against a hotel and rubbing the half-moons on his nails with a silk handkerchief.

"Paresis or *superannuated*?" I asks him.

"Hello, Billy," says Silver; "I'm glad to see you. Yes, it seemed to me that the West was accumulating a little too much wiseness. I've been saving New York for dessert. I know it's a low-down trick to take things from these people. They only know this and that and pass to and fro and think ever and anon. I'd hate for my mother to know I was skinning these weak-minded ones. She raised me better."

"Is there a crush already in the waiting rooms of the old doctor that does skin *grafting*?" I asks.

"Well, no," says Silver; "you needn't back Epidermis to win today. I've only been here a month. But I'm ready to begin; and the members of Willie Manhattan's Sunday School class, each of whom has volunteered to contribute a portion of cuticle toward this *rehabilitation*, may as well send their photos to the *Evening Daily*.

"I've been studying the town," says Silver, "and reading the papers every day, and I know it as well as the cat in the City Hall knows an O'Sullivan. People here lie down on the floor and scream and kick when you are the least bit slow about taking money from them. Come up in my room and I'll tell you. We'll work the town together, Billy, for the sake of old times."

Swindling - *Cheating*
Superannuated - *Retired because of age*
Grafting - *Implanting, transplanting*
Rehabilitation - *Restore to a condition of good health*

Silver takes me up in a hotel. He has a quantity of irrelevant objects lying about.

"There's more ways of getting money from these metropolitan *hayseeds*," says Silver, "than there is of cooking rice in Charleston, S. C. They'll bite at anything. The brains of most of 'em commute. The wiser they are in intelligence the less perception of *cognizance* they have. Why, didin't a man the other day sell J. P. Morgan an oil portrait of Rockefeller, Jr., for Andrea del Sarto's celebrated painting of the young Saint John!

"You see that bundle of printed stuff in the corner, Billy? That's gold mining stock. I started out one day to sell that, but I quit it in two hours. Why? Got arrested for blocking the street. People fought to buy it. I sold the policeman a block of it on the way to the station-house, and then I took it off the market. I don't want people to give me their money. I want some little consideration connected with the transaction to keep my pride from being hurt. I want 'em to guess the missing letter in Chic-go, or draw to a pair of nines before they pay me a cent of money.

"Now there's another little scheme that worked so easy I had to quit it. You see that bottle of blue ink on the table? I tattooed an anchor on the back of my hand and went to a bank and told 'em I was Admiral Dewey's nephew. They offered to cash my draft on him for a thousand, but I didn't know my uncle's first name. It shows, though, what an easy town it is. As for burglars, they won't go in a house now unless there's a hot supper ready and a few college students to wait on 'em. They're slugging citizens all over the upper part of the city and I guess, taking the town from end to end, it's a plain case of *assault* and Battery."

"Monty," says I, when Silver had *slacked*, up, "you may have Manhattan correctly discriminated in your perorative, but I doubt it. I've only been in town two hours, but it don't dawn upon me that it's ours with a cherry in it. There ain't enough rus in urbe about it to suit me. I'd be a good deal much better satisfied if the citizens had a straw or more in their hair, and run more to *velveteen* vests and buckeye watch charms. They don't look easy to me."

"You've got it, Billy," says Silver. "All emigrants have it. New York's bigger than Little Rock or Europe, and it frightens a foreigner. You'll be all right. I tell you I feel like slapping

Hayseeds - *Seeds*
Cognizance -
Awareness
Assault - *A sudden*
Slacked - *Loosened*
Velveteen - *A cotton fabric resembling velvet*

the people here because they don't send me all their money in laundry baskets, with **germicide** sprinkled over it. I hate to go down on the street to get it. Who wears the diamonds in this town? Why, Winnie, the Wiretapper's wife, and Bella, the Buncosteerer's bride. New Yorkers can be worked easier than a blue rose on a tidy. The only thing that bothers me is I know I'll break the cigars in my vest pocket when I get my clothes all full of twenties."

"I hope you are right, Monty," says I; "but I wish all the same I had been satisfied with a small business in Little Rock. The crop of farmers is never so short out there but what you can get a few of 'em to sign a petition for a new post office that you can discount for $200 at the county bank. The people hear appear to possess **instincts** of **self-preservation** and il-liberality. I fear me that we are not cultured enough to tackle this game."

"Don't worry," says Silver. "I've got this Jayville-near-Tarrytown correctly estimated as sure as North River is the Hudson and East River ain't a river. Why, there are people living in four blocks of Broadway who never saw any kind of a building except a **skyscraper** in their lives! A good, live hustling Western man ought to get conspicuous enough here inside of three months to incur either Jerome's **clemency** or Lawson's displeasure."

"Hyperbole aside," says I, "do you know of any immediate system of **buncoing** the community out of a dollar or two except by applying to the Salvation Army or having a fit on Miss Helen Gould's doorsteps?"

"Dozens of 'em," says Silver. "How much capital have you got, Billy?"

"A thousand," I told him.

"I've got $1,200," says he. "We'll pool and do a big piece of business. There's so many ways we can make a million that I don't know how to begin."

The next morning Silver meets me at the hotel and he is all **sonorous** and stirred with a kind of silent joy.

"We're to meet J. P. Morgan this afternoon," says he. "A man I know in the hotel wants to introduce us. He's a friend of his. He says he likes to meet people from the West."

"That sounds nice and **plausible**," says I. "I'd like to know Mr. Morgan."

Germicide -*Any substance that kills germs*
Instincts - *Natural intuitive power*
Sonorous - *Loud, deep*
Plausible - *Well-spoken*

"It won't hurt us a bit," says Silver, "to get *acquainted* with a few finance kings. I kind of like the social way New York has with strangers."

The man Silver knew was named Klein. At three o'clock Klein brought his Wall Street friend to see us in Silver's room. "Mr. Morgan" looked some like his pictures, and he had a Turkish towel wrapped around his left foot, and he walked with a cane.

"Mr. Silver and Mr. Pescud," says Klein. "It sounds *superfluous*," says he, "to mention the name of the greatest financial -"

"Cut it out, Klein," says Mr. Morgan. "I'm glad to know you gents; I take great interest in the West. Klein tells me you're from Little Rock. I think I've a railroad or two out there somewhere. If either of you guys would like to deal a hand or two of stud poker I -"

"Now, Pierpont," cuts in Klein, "you forget!"

"Excuse me, gents!" says Morgan; "since I've had the gout so bad I sometimes play a social game of cards at my house. Neither of you never knew One-eyed Peters, did you, while you was around Little Rock? He lived in Seattle, New Mexico."

Before we could answer, Mr. Morgan hammers on the floor with his can and begins to walk up and down, swearing in a loud tone of voice.

"They have been *pounding* your stocks to-day on the Street, Pierpont?" asks Klein, smiling.

"Stocks! No!" roars Mr. Morgan. "It's that picture I sent an agent to Europe to buy. I just thought about it. He cabled me to-day that it ain't to be found in all Italy. I'd pay $50,000 to-morrow for that picture - yes, $75,000. I give the agent a la carte in purchasing it. I cannot understand why the art galleries will allow a De Vinchy to -"

"Why, Mr. Morgan," says klein; "I thought you owned all of the De Vinchy paintings."

"What is the picture like, Mr. Morgan?" asks Silver. "It must be as big as the side of the Flatiron Building."

"I'm afraid your art education is on the bum, Mr. Silver," says Morgan. "The picture is 27 inches by 42; and it is called 'Love's Idle Hour.' It represents a number of cloak models doing the two-step on the bank of a purple river. The *cablegram*

Acquainted
- To make, more/less familiar
Superfluous - Being more than sufficient
Pounding - To strike repeatedly with great force

said it might have been brought to this country. My collection will never be complete without that picture. Well, so long, gents; us financiers must keep early hours."

Mr. Morgan and Klein went away together in a cab. Me and Silver talked about how simple and unsuspecting great people was; and Silver said what a shame it would be to try to rob a man like Mr. Morgan; and I said I thought it would be rather imprudent, myself. Klein proposes a stroll after dinner; and me and him and Silver walks down toward Seventh Avenue to see the sights. Klein sees a pair of cuff links that instigate his admiration in a *pawnshop* window, and we all go in while he buys 'em.

After we got back to the hotel and Klein had gone, Silver jumps at me and waves his hands.

"Did you see it?" says he. "Did you see it, Billy?"

"What?" I asks.

"Why, that picture that Morgan wants. It's hanging in that pawnshop, behind the desk. I didn't say anything because Klein was there. It's the article sure as you live. The girls are as natural as paint can make them, all measuring 36 and 25 and 42 skirts, if they had any skirts, and they're doing a buck-and-wing on the bank of a river with the blues. What did Mr. Morgan say he'd give for it? Oh, don't make me tell you. They can't know what it is in that pawnshop."

When the pawnshop opened the next morning me and Silver was standing there as anxious as if we wanted to soak our Sunday suit to buy a drink. We sauntered inside, and began to look at watch-chains.

"That's a violent specimen of a chromo you've got up there," remarked Silver, casual, to the pawnbroker. "But I kind of *enthuse* over the girl with the shoulderblades and red bunting. Would an offer of $2.25 for it cause you to knock over any *fragile* articles of your stock in hurrying it off the nail?"

The pawnbroker smiles and goes on showing us plate watch-chains.

Pawnshop - *Premisens*
Enthuse - *To become enthusiastic*
Fragile - *Delicate*
Unredeemed - *To buy*

"That picture," says he, "was pledged a year ago by an Italian gentleman. I loaned him $500 on it. It is called 'Love's Idle Hour,' and it is by Leonardo de Vinchy. Two days ago the legal time expired, and it became an *unredeemed* pledge. Here is a style of chain that is worn a great deal now."

At the end of half an hour, me and Silver paid the *pawn-broker* $2,000 and walked out with the picture. Silver got into a *cab* with it and started for Morgan's office. I goes to the hotel and waits for him. In two hours, Silver comes back.

"Did you see Mr. Morgan?" I asks. "How much did he pay you for it?"

Silver sits down and *fools* with a *tassel* on the table cover.

"I never exactly saw Mr. Morgan," he says, "because Mr. Morgan's been in Europe for a month. But what's worrying me, Billy, is this: The *department stores* have all got that same picture on sale, framed, for $3.48. And they charge $3.50 for the frame alone - that's what I can't understand."

Food For Thought

Mr. Morgan was one of the few finance kings of New York according to Silver. What did Morgan want to buy and how did he fool Billy and Silver (both) at the end of the story? Can you suggest a moral for the story? Also give appropriate reasons for your suggestion.

Cab - *Taxi*
Tassel - *A pendant ornament tied to a piece*
Department stores - *Big retail shops, grocery of thread*

The Ransom Of Red Chief

IT looked like a good thing: but wait till I tell you. We were down South, in Alabama - Bill Driscoll and myself- when this kidnapping idea struck us. It was, as Bill afterward expressed it, "during a moment of temporary mental apparition"; but we didn't find that out till later.

There was a town down there, as flat as a flannel-cake, and called Summit, of course. It contained inhabitants of as undeleterious and self-satisfied a class of peasantry as ever clustered around a Maypole.

Bill and me had a joint capital of about six hundred dollars, and we needed just two thousand dollars more to pull off a *fraudulent* town-lot scheme in Western Illinois with. We talked it over on the front steps of the hotel. *Philoprogenitiveness*, says we, is strong in semi-rural communities therefore, and for other reasons, a kidnapping project ought to do better there than in the radius of newspapers that send reporters out in plain clothes to stir up talk about such things. We knew that Summit couldn't get after us with anything stronger than constables and, maybe, some *lackadaisical bloodhounds* and a *diatribe* or two in the *Weekly Farmers' Budget*. So, it looked good.

We selected for our victim the only child of a prominent citizen named Ebenezer Dorset. The father was respectable and tight, a *mortgage* fancier and a stern, upright collection-plate passer and forecloser. The kid was a boy of ten, with bas-relief *freckles*, and hair the colour of the cover of the magazine you buy at the news-stand when you want to catch a train. Bill and me figured that Ebenezer would melt down for a ransom of two thousand dollars to a cent. But wait till I tell you.

About two miles from Summit was a little mountain, covered with a dense cedar brake. On the rear elevation of this mountain was a cave. There we stored provisions.

One evening after sundown, we drove in a *buggy* past old Dorset's house. The kid was in the street, throwing rocks at a kitten on the opposite fence.

"Hey, little boy!" says Bill, "would you like to have a bag of candy and a nice ride?"

Clustered - *Crowded*
Fraudulnt - *Put together*
Lackadaisical - *Without interest*
Diatribe - *A bitter, sharp attacj*
Mortgage - *To pledge as security*
Trickles - *To flow*
Buggy - *A light*

The boy catches Bill neatly in the eye with a piece of brick.

"That will cost the old man an extra five hundred dollars," says Bill, climbing over the wheel.

That boy put up a fight like a welter-weight cinnamon bear; but, at last, we got him down in the bottom of the buggy and drove away. We took him up to the cave, and I hitched the horse in the cedar brake. After dark I drove the buggy to the little village, three miles away, where we had hired it, and walked back to the mountain.

Bill was pasting *court-plaster* over the scratches and bruises on his features. There was a fire burning behind the big rock at the entrance of the cave, and the boy was watching a pot of boiling coffee, with two *buzzard* tailfeathers stuck in his red hair. He points a stick at me when I come up, and says:

"Ha! cursed paleface, do you dare to enter the camp of Red Chief, the terror of the plains?"

"He's all right now," says Bill, rolling up his trousers and examining some bruises on his *shins*. "We're playing Indian. We're making Buffalo Bill's show look like magic-lantern views of Palestine in the town hall. I'm Old Hank, the Trapper, Red Chief's captive, and I'm to be scalped at daybreak. By Geronimo! that kid can kick hard."

Yes, sir, that boy seemed to be having the time of his life. The fun of camping out in a cave had made him forget that he was a captive himself. He immediately christened me Snake-eye, the Spy, and announced that, when his braves returned from the warpath, I was to be *broiled* at the stake at the rising of the sun.

Then we had supper; and he filled his mouth full of *bacon* and bread and gravy, and began to talk. He made a during-dinner speech something like this:

"I like this fine. I never camped out before; but I had a pet 'possum once, and I was nine last birthday. I hate to go to school. Rats ate up sixteen of Jimmy Talbot's aunt's *speckled* hen's eggs. Are there any real Indians in these woods? I want some more gravy. Does the trees moving make the wind blow? We had five puppies. What makes your nose so red, Hank? My father has lots of money. Are the stars hot? I whipped Ed Walker twice, Saturday. I don't like girls. You dassent catch toads unless with a string. Do oxen make any noise? Why are oranges round? Have you got beds to sleep on in this cave?

Buzzard - *Senseless*
Shins - *The front part of the leg from the knee to the ankle*
Broiled - *To cook by direct heat*
Bacon - *Meat of a pig*
Speckled - *Spots/ marks on the skin*

Amos Murray has got six toes. A parrot can talk, but a monkey or a fish can't. How many does it take to make twelve?"

Every few minutes he would remember that he was a pesky redskin, and pick up his stick rifle and *tiptoe* to the mouth of the cave to rubber for the scouts of the hated paleface. Now and then he would let out a warwhoop that made Old Hank the Trapper, shiver. That boy had Bill terrorised from the start.

"Red Chief," says I to the kid, "would you like to go home?"

"Aw, what for?" says he. "I don't have any fun at home. I hate to go to school. I like to camp out. You won't take me back home again, Snake-eye, will you?"

"Not right away," says I. "We'll stay here in the cave a while."

"All right!" says he. "That'll be fine. I never had such fun in all my life."

We went to bed about eleven o'clock. We spread down some wide blankets and quilts and put Red Chief between us. We weren't afraid he'd run away. He kept us awake for three hours, jumping up and reaching for his rifle and screeching: "Hist! pard," in mine and Bill's ears, as the fancied *crackle* of a twig or the rustle of a leaf revealed to his young imagination the stealthy approach of the *outlaw* band. At last, I fell into a troubled sleep, and dreamed that I had been kidnapped and chained to a tree by a *ferocious* pirate with red hair.

Just at daybreak, I was awakened by a series of awful screams from Bill. They weren't yells, or howls, or shouts, or whoops, or yawps, such as you'd expect from a manly set of vocal organs - they were simply indecent, terrifying, humiliating screams, such as women emit when they see ghosts or caterpillars. It's an awful thing to hear a strong, *desperate*, fat man scream *incontinently* in a cave at daybreak.

I jumped up to see what the matter was. Red Chief was sitting on Bill's chest, with one hand *twined* in Bill's hair. In the other he had the sharp case-knife we used for slicing bacon; and he was industriously and realistically trying to take Bill's scalp, according to the sentence that had been pronounced upon him the evening before.

I got the knife away from the kid and made him lie down again. But, from that moment, Bill's spirit was broken. He laid

Tiptoe - *To move slowly*
Ferocious - *Fierce, very cruel*
Incontinently - *Immediately*
Twined - *Coiled/ twisted*

down on his side of the bed, but he never closed an eye again in sleep as long as that boy was with us. I dozed off for a while, but along toward sun-up I remembered that Red Chief had said I was to be burned at the stake at the rising of the sun. I wasn't nervous or afraid; but I sat up and lit my pipe and leaned against a rock.

"What you getting up so soon for, Sam?" asked Bill.

"Me?" says I. "Oh, I got a kind of a pain in my shoulder. I thought sitting up would rest it."

"You're a liar!" says Bill. "You're afraid. You was to be burned at sunrise, and you was afraid he'd do it. And he would, too, if he could find a match. Ain't it awful, Sam? Do you think anybody will pay out money to get a little imp like that back home?"

"Sure," said I. "A rowdy kid like that is just the kind that parents dote on. Now, you and the Chief get up and cook breakfast, while I go up on the top of this mountain and *reconnoitre*."

I went up on the peak of the little mountain and ran my eye over the *contiguous vicinity*. Over toward Summit I expected to see the sturdy *yeomanry* of the village armed with scythes and *pitchforks* beating the countryside for the dastardly kidnappers. But what I saw was a peaceful landscape dotted with one man ploughing with a dun mule. Nobody was dragging the creek; no couriers dashed hither and yon, bringing tidings of no news to the *distracted* parents. There was a *sylvan* attitude of somnolent sleepiness pervading that section of the external outward surface of Alabama that lay exposed to my view. "Perhaps," says I to myself, "it has not yet been discovered that the wolves have borne away the tender lambkin from the fold. Heaven help the wolves!" says I, and I went down the mountain to breakfast.

When I got to the cave I found Bill backed up against the side of it, breathing hard, and the boy threatening to smash him with a rock half as big as a coconut.

"He put a red-hot boiled potato down my back," explained Bill, "and then mashed it with his foot; and I boxed his ears. Have you got a gun about you, Sam?"

I took the rock away from the boy and kind of patched up the argument. "I'll fix you," says the kid to Bill. "No man ever yet struck the Red Chief but what he got paid for it. You better beware!"

Reconnoitre - *To survey/inspect*
Contiguous - *In close proximity*
Vicinity - *Surrounding area*
Distracted - *Attention diverted*

Best Stories of O.Henry

After breakfast the kid takes a piece of leather with strings wrapped around it out of his pocket and goes outside the cave *unwinding* it.

"What's he up to now?" says Bill, anxiously. "You don't think he'll run away, do you, Sam?"

"No fear of it," says I. "He don't seem to be much of a home body. But we've got to fix up some plan about the ransom. There don't seem to be much excitement around Summit on account of his disappearance; but maybe they haven't realised yet that he's gone. His folks may think he's spending the night with Aunt Jane or one of the neighbours. Anyhow, he'll be missed to-day. To-night we must get a message to his father demanding the two thousand dollars for his return."

Just then we heard a kind of *war-whoop*, such as David might have emitted when he knocked out the champion Goliath. It was a sling that Red Chief had pulled out of his pocket, and he was whirling it around his head.

I dodged, and heard a heavy thud and a kind of a sigh from Bill, like a horse gives out when you take his saddle off. A *niggerhead* rock the size of an egg had caught Bill just behind his left ear. He loosened himself all over and fell in the fire across the frying pan of hot water for washing the dishes. I dragged him out and poured cold water on his head for half an hour.

By and by, Bill sits up and feels behind his ear and says: "Sam, do you know who my favourite Biblical character is?"

"Take it easy," says I. "You'll come to your senses presently."

"King Herod," says he. "You won't go away and leave me here alone, will you, Sam?"

I went out and caught that boy and shook him until his *freckles rattled.*

"If you don't behave," says I, "I'll take you straight home. Now, are you going to be good, or not?"

"I was only funning," says he *sullenly*. "I didn't mean to hurt Old Hank. But what did he hit me for? I'll behave, Snake-eye, if you won't send me home, and if you'll let me play the Black Scout to-day."

"I don't know the game," says I. "That's for you and Mr. Bill to decide. He's your playmate for the day. I'm going

War-whoop - *A yell uttered while attacking during war*
Niggerhead - *A strong, black chewing*
Freckles - *Small brownish spots on skin*
Rattled - *To talk rapidly*
Sullenly - *Gloomily, morose*

away for a while, on business. Now, you come in and make friends with him and say you are sorry for hurting him, or home you go, at once."

I made him and Bill shake hands, and then I took Bill aside and told him I was going to Poplar Cove, a little village three miles from the cave, and find out what I could about how the kidnapping had been regarded in Summit. Also, I thought it best to send a *peremptory* letter to old man Dorset that day, demanding the ransom and dictating how it should be paid.

"You know, Sam," says Bill, "I've stood by you without batting an eye in earthquakes, fire and flood - in poker games, dynamite *outrages*, police raids, train robberies and cyclones. I never lost my nerve yet till we kidnapped that two-legged skyrocket of a kid. He's got me going. You won't leave me long with him, will you, Sam?"

"I'll be back some time this afternoon," says I. "You must keep the boy amused and quiet till I return. And now we'll write the letter to old Dorset."

Bill and I got paper and pencil and worked on the letter while Red Chief, with a blanket wrapped around him, *strutted* up and down, guarding the mouth of the cave. Bill begged me tearfully to make the ransom fifteen hundred dollars instead of two thousand. "I ain't attempting," says he, "to decry the celebrated moral aspect of parental affection, but we're dealing with humans, and it ain't human for anybody to give up two thousand dollars for that forty-pound chunk of freckled wildcat. I'm willing to take a chance at fifteen hundred dollars. You can charge the difference up to me."

So, to relieve Bill, I acceded, and we *collaborated* a letter that ran this way:

Ebenezer Dorset, Esq.:

We have your boy concealed in a place far from Summit. It is useless for you or the most skilful detectives to attempt to find him. Absolutely, the only terms on which you can have him restored to you are these: We demand fifteen hundred dollars in large bills for his return; the money to be left at midnight to-night at the same spot and in the same box as your reply - as hereinafter described. If you agree to these terms, send your answer in writing by a solitary messenger to-night at half-past eight o'clock. After crossing Owl Creek, on the road to Poplar

Peremptory
- Leaving no opportunity for refusal
Outrages - *Insults*
Strutted - *To walk with vain/pride*
Collaborated - *To work with one another*

Cove, there are three large trees about a hundred yards apart, close to the fence of the wheat field on the right-hand side. At the bottom of the fence-post, opposite the third tree, will be found a small *pasteboard box.*

The messenger will place the answer in this box and return immediately to Summit.

If you attempt any *treachery* or fail to comply with our demand as stated, you will never see your boy again.

If you pay the money as demanded, he will be returned to you safe and well within three hours. These terms are final, and if you do not accede to them no further communication will be attempted.

TWO DESPERATE MEN.

I addressed this letter to Dorset, and put it in my pocket. As I was about to start, the kid comes up to me and says:

"Aw, Snake-eye, you said I could play the Black Scout while you was gone."

"Play it, of course," says I. "Mr. Bill will play with you. What kind of a game is it?"

"I'm the Black Scout," says Red Chief, "and I have to ride to the *stockade* to warn the settlers that the Indians are coming. I'm tired of playing Indian myself. I want to be the Black Scout."

"All right," says I. "It sounds harmless to me. I guess Mr. Bill will help you foil the pesky savages."

"What am I to do?" asks Bill, looking at the kid suspiciously.

"You are the hoss," says Black Scout. "Get down on your hands and knees. How can I ride to the stockade without a hoss?"

"You'd better keep him interested," said I, "till we get the scheme going. Loosen up."

Bill gets down on his all fours, and a look comes in his eye like a rabbit's when you catch it in a trap.

" How far is it to the stockade, kid? " he asks, in a husky manner of voice.

"Ninety miles," says the Black Scout. "And you have to hump yourself to get there on time. Whoa, now!"

The Black Scout jumps on Bill's back and digs his heels in his side.

Stockage - *An enclosure/barrier*
Hump - *A rounded protuberance*
Suspiciously - *Doubtful dubious*

"For Heaven's sake," says Bill, "hurry back, Sam, as soon as you can. I wish we hadn't made the ransom more than a thousand. Say, you quit kicking me or I 'll get up and warm you good."

I walked over to Poplar Cove and sat around the post office and store, talking with the chawbacons that came in to trade. One *whiskerand* says that he hears Summit is all upset on account of Elder Ebenezer Dorset's boy having been lost or stolen. That was all I wanted to know. I bought some smoking tobacco, referred casually to the price of black-eyed peas, posted my letter *surreptitiously* and came away. The postmaster said the mail-carrier would come by in an hour to take the mail on to Summit.

When I got back to the cave Bill and the boy were not to be found. I explored the *vicinity* of the cave, and risked a yodel or two, but there was no response.

So I lighted my pipe and sat down on a mossy bank to await developments.

In about half an hour I heard the bushes rustle, and Bill wabbled out into the little glade in front of the cave. Behind him was the kid, stepping softly like a scout, with a broad grin on his face. Bill stopped, took off his hat and wiped his face with a red handkerchief. The kid stopped about eight feet behind him.

"Sam," says Bill, "I suppose you'll think I'm a renegade, but I couldn't help it. I'm a grown person with masculine proclivities and habits of self-defence, but there is a time when all systems of *egotism* and *predominance* fail. The boy is gone. I have sent him home. All is off. There was martyrs in old times," goes on Bill, "that suffered death rather than give up the particular graft they enjoyed. None of 'em ever was subjugated to such supernatural tortures as I have been. I tried to be faithful to our articles of depredation; but there came a limit."

"What's the trouble, Bill?" I asks him.

"I was rode," says Bill, "the ninety miles to the stockade, not barring an inch. Then, when the settlers was rescued, I was given oats. Sand ain't a *palatable* substitute. And then, for an hour I had to try to explain to him why there was nothin' in holes, how a road can run both ways and what makes the grass green. I tell you, Sam, a human can only stand so much. I takes him by the neck of his clothes and drags him down the

Whisked - *Having whiskers/hair on the face*
Surreptitously - *Secretly*
Egotism - *Boast fullness*
Palatable - *Tasty, acceptable*

mountain. On the way he kicks my legs black-and-blue from the knees down; and I've got two or three bites on my thumb and hand *cauterised*.

"But he's gone" - continues Bill - "gone home. I showed him the road to Summit and kicked him about eight feet nearer there at one kick. I'm sorry we lose the ransom; but it was either that or Bill Driscoll to the madhouse."

Bill is *puffing* and blowing, but there is a look of *ineffable* peace and growing content on his rose-pink features.

"Bill," says I, "there isn't any heart disease in your family, is there?"

"No," says Bill, "nothing chronic except malaria and accidents. Why?"

"Then you might turn around," says I, "and have a look behind you."

Bill turns and sees the boy, and loses his complexion and sits down plump on the ground and begins to pluck aimlessly at grass and little sticks. For an hour I was afraid for his mind. And then I told him that my scheme was to put the whole job through immediately and that we would get the ransom and be off with it by midnight if old Dorset fell in with our proposition. So Bill braced up enough to give the kid a weak sort of a smile and a promise to play the Russian in a Japanese war with him as soon as he felt a little better.

I had a scheme for collecting that ransom without danger of being caught by *counterplots* that ought to commend itself to professional kidnappers. The tree under which the answer was to be left - and the money later on - was close to the road fence with big, bare fields on all sides. If a gang of constables should be watching for any one to come for the note they could see him a long way off crossing the fields or in the road. But no, sirree! At half-past eight, I was up in that tree as well hidden as a tree toad, waiting for the messenger to arrive.

Exactly on time, a half-grown boy rides up the road on a bicycle, locates the pasteboard box at the foot of the fencepost, slips a folded piece of paper into it and pedals away again back toward Summit.

I waited an hour and then concluded the thing was square. I slid down the tree, got the note, slipped along the fence till I struck the woods, and was back at the cave in another half an hour. I opened the note, got near the lantern and read it to

Cauterised - *To burn with a hot iron*
Puffing - *Inhaling/ exhaling*
Ineffable -*Inexpressible*
Counterplots - *To oppose*

Bill. It was written with a pen in a crabbed hand, and the sum and substance of it was this:

Two Desperate Men.

Gentlemen: I received your letter to-day by post, in regard to the ransom you ask for the return of my son. I think you are a little high in your demands, and I hereby make you a counter-proposition, which I am inclined to believe you will accept. You bring Johnny home and pay me two hundred and fifty dollars in cash, and I agree to take him off your hands. You had better come at night, for the neighbours believe he is lost, and I couldn't be responsible for what they would do to anybody they saw bringing him back.

Very respectfully,
Ebenezer Dorset.

"Great pirates of Penzance!" says I; "of all the *impudent* - "

But I glanced at Bill, and hesitated. He had the most appealing look in his eyes I ever saw on the face of a dumb or a talking brute.

"Sam," says he, "what's two hundred and fifty dollars, after all? We've got the money. One more night of this kid will send me to a bed in Bedlam. Besides being a thorough gentleman, I think Mr. Dorset is a *spendthrift* for making us such a liberal offer. You ain't going to let the chance go, are you?"

"Tell you the truth, Bill," says I, "this little he ewe lamb has somewhat got on my nerves too. We'll take him home, pay the ransom and make our get-away."

We took him home that night. We got him to go by telling him that his father had bought a silver-mounted rifle and a pair of *moccasins* for him, and we were going to hunt bears the next day.

It was just twelve o'clock when we knocked at Ebenezer's front door. Just at the moment when I should have been abstracting the fifteen hundred dollars from the box under the tree, according to the original proposition, Bill was counting out two hundred and fifty dollars into Dorset's hand.

When the kid found out we were going to leave him at home he started up a howl like a *calliope* and fastened himself as tight as a leech to Bill's leg. His father peeled him away gradually, like a porous plaster.

Impudent -
Shameless, immodest
Spendthrift -
Extravagant
Moccasins - *Hard-soled shoes*
Calliope - *A steam-whistle organ in music with a loud sound*

"How long can you hold him?" asks Bill.

"I'm not as strong as I used to be," says old Dorset, "but I think I can promise you ten minutes."

"Enough," says Bill. "In ten minutes I shall cross the Central, Southern and Middle Western States, and be legging it *trippingly* for the Canadian border."

And, as dark as it was, and as fat as Bill was, and as good a runner as I am, he was a good mile and a half out of Summit before I could catch up with him.

Trippingly -

Food For Thought

Do you think that this story, 'The Ransom of the Red Chief' written by O.Henry in 1910 is one of his best works and one of the most humourous stories of the world? Give reasons for your answer.

A Ramble In Aphasia

MY wife and I parted on that morning in precisely our usual manner. She left her second cup of tea to follow me to the front door. There she plucked from my *lapel* the invisible strand of lint (the universal act of woman to proclaim ownership) and bade me to take care of my cold. I had no cold. Next came her kiss of parting - the lever kiss of domesticity flavored with Young Hyson. There was no fear of the *extemporaneous*, of variety spicing her infinite custom. With the deft touch of long *malpractice*, she dabbed awry my well-set scarf pin; and then, as I closed the door, I heard her morning slippers pattering back to her cooling tea.

When I set out I had no thought or premonition of what was to occur. The attack came suddenly. For many weeks I had been toiling, almost night and day, at a famous railroad law case that I won triumphantly but a few days previously. In fact, I had been digging away at the law almost without *cessation* for many years. Once or twice good Doctor Volney, my friend and physician, had warned me.

"If you don't slacken up, Belford," he said, "you'll go suddenly to pieces. Either your nerves or your brain will give way. Tell me, does a week pass in which you do not read in the papers of a case of *aphasia* - of some man lost, wandering nameless, with his past and his identity blotted out - and all from that little brain clot made by overwork or worry?"

"I always thought," said I, "that the clot in those instances was really to be found on the brains of the newspaper reporters."

Doctor Volney shook his head.

"The disease exists," he said. "You need a change or a rest. Court-room, office and home - there is the only route you travel. For recreation you - read law books. Better take warning in time."

"On Thursday nights," I said, defensively, "my wife and I play *cribbage*. On Sundays she reads to me the weekly letter from her mother. That law books are not a recreation remains yet to be established."

Lapel - *The continuation of the turned*
Extemporaneous - *Spontaneous*
Malpractice - *Improper*
Aphasia - *Loss ability to speak*
Cribbage - *A card game for two*

That morning as I walked I was thinking of Doctor Volney's words. I was feeling as well as I usually did - possibly in better spirits than usual.

I woke with stiff and cramped muscles from having slept long on the *incommodious* seat of a day coach. I leaned my head against the seat and tried to think. After a long time I said to myself: "I must have a name of some sort." I searched my pockets. Not a card; not a letter; not a paper or *monogram* could I find. But I found in my coat pocket nearly $3,000 in bills of large denomination. "I must be some one, of course," I repeated to myself, and began again to consider.

The car was well crowded with men, among whom, I told myself, there must have been some common interest, for they intermingled freely, and seemed in the best good humor and spirits. One of them - a stout, spectacled gentleman enveloped in a decided odor of *cinnamon* and aloes - took the vacant half of my seat with a friendly nod, and unfolded a newspaper. In the intervals between his periods of reading, we conversed, as travelers will, on current affairs. I found myself able to sustain the conversation on such subjects with credit, at least to my memory. By and by my companion said:

"You are one of us, of course. Fine lot of men the West sends in this time. I'm glad they held the convention in New York; I've never been East before. My name's R. P. Bolder -

Bolder & Son, of Hickory Grove, Missouri."

Though unprepared, I rose to the emergency, as men will when put to it. Now must I hold a christening, and be at once babe, parson and parent. My senses came to the rescue of my slower brain. The insistent odor of drugs from my compainion supplied one idea; a glance at his newspaper, where my eye met a *conspicuous* advertisement, assisted me further.

"My name," said I, glibly, "is Edward Pinkhammer. I am a druggist, and my home is in Cornopolis, Kansas."

"I knew you were a druggist," said my fellow traveler, affably. "I saw the callous spot on your right forefinger where the handle of the pestle rubs. Of course, you are a delegate to our National Convention."

"Are all these men druggists?" I asked, wonderingly.

Incommodious
- *Troublesome, inconvenient*
Monogram - *A design of one*
Cinnamon - *A Indian spice*
Pharmaceutists - *Druggists, chemists*

"They are. This car came through from the West. And they're your old-time druggists, too - none of your patent tablet-and-granule *pharmaceutists* that use slot machines instead of a *prescription* desk. We percolate our own paregoric and roll our own pills, and we ain't above handling a few garden seeds in the spring, and carrying a side line of confectionery and shoes.

I tell you Hampinker, I've got an idea to spring on this convention - new ideas is what they want. Now, you know the shelf bottles of *Tartar emetic* and *Rochelle salt* Ant. et Pot. Tart. and Sod. et Pot. Tart. - one's poison, you know, and the other's harmless. It's easy to mistake one label for the other. Where do druggists mostly keep 'em? Why, as far apart as possible, on different shelves. That's wrong. I say keep 'em side by side, so when you want one you can always compare it with the other and avoid mistakes. Do you catch the idea?"

"It seems to me a very good one," I said.

"All right! When I spring it on the convention you back it up. We'll make some of these Eastern orange-phosphate-and-massage-cream professors that think they're the only *lozenges* in the market look like *hypodermic* tablets."

"If I can be of any aid," I said, warming, "the two bottles of - er -"

"Tartrate of antimony and potash, and tartrate of soda and potash."

"Shall henceforth sit side by side," I concluded, firmly.

"Now, there's another thing," said Mr. Bolder. "For an excipient in *manipulating* a pill mass which do you prefer - the magnesia carbonate or the pulverised glycerrhiza radix?"

"The - er - magnesia," I said. It was easier to say than the other word.

Mr. Bolder glanced at me distrustfully through his spectacles.

"Give me the glycerrhiza," said he. "Magnesia cakes."

"Here's another one of these fake aphasia cases," he said, presently, handing me his newspaper, and laying his finger upon an article. "I don't believe in 'em. I put nine out of ten of 'em down as frauds. A man gets sick of his business and his folks and wants to have a good time. He skips out somewhere,

Prescription - *Written instructions form a physician*
Tartar emetic - *Another name for antimony potassium tartrate*
Rochelle salt - *A colourless, white, water soluble soled*
Lozenges - *Toffees*
Hypodermic - *Under the skin*

and when they find him he pretends to have lost his memory - don't know his own name, and won't even recognize the strawberry mark on his wife's left shoulder. Aphasia! Tut! Why can't they stay at home and forget?"

I took the paper and read, after the pungent headlines, the following:

"DENVER, June 12. - Elwyn C. Belford, a prominent lawyer, is mysteriously missing from his home since three days ago, and all efforts to locate him have been in vain. Mr. Bellford is a well-known citizen of the highest standing, and has enjoyed a large and *lucrative* law practice. He is married and owns a fine home and the most extensive private library in the State. On the day of his disappearance, he drew quite a large sum of money from his bank.

No one can be found who saw him after he left the bank. Mr. Bellford was a man of singularly quiet and domestic tastes, and seemed to find his happiness in his home and profession. If any clue at all exists to his strange disappearance, it my be found in the fact that for some months he has been deeply absorbed in an important law case in connection with the Q. Y. and Z. Railroad Company. It is feared that overwork may have affected his mind. Every effort is being made to discover the whereabouts of the missing man."

"It seems to me you are not altogether uncynical, Mr. Bolder," I said, after I had read the despatch. "This has the sound, to me, of a genuine case. Why should this man, prosperous, happily married, and respected, choose suddenly to abandon everything? I know that these lapses of memory do occur, and that men do find themselves *adrift* without a name, a history or a home."

"Oh, gammon and jalap!" said Mr. Bolder. "It's larks they're after. There's too much education nowadays. Men know about aphasia, and they use it for an excuse. The women are wise, too. When it's all over they look you in the eye, as scientific as you please, and say: 'He hypnotised me.'"

Thus Mr. Bolder *diverted*, but did not aid, me with his comments and philosophy.

Lucrative - *Profitable*
Adrift - *Floating without, control*
Diverted - *Deflected, distracted*
Buoyancy - *The power to float*

We arrived in New York about ten at night. I rode in a cab to a hotel, and I wrote my name "Edward Pinkhammer" in the register. As I did so I felt pervade me a splendid, wild, intoxicating *buoyancy* - a sense of unlimited freedom, of newly attained possibilities. I was just born into the world. The old fetters - whatever they had been - were stricken from my hands and feet. The future lay before me a clear road such as an infant enters, and I could set out upon it equipped with a man's learning and experience.

I thought the hotel clerk looked at me five seconds too long. I had no baggage.

"The Druggists' *Convention*," I said. "My trunk has somehow failed to arrive." I drew out a roll of money.

"Ah!" said he, showing an *auriferous* tooth, "we have quite a number of the Western delegates stopping here." He struck a bell for the boy.

I endeavoured to give color to my role.

"There is an important movement on foot among us Westerners," I said, "in regard to a recommendation to the convention that the bottles containing the tartrate of antimony and potash, and the tartrate of sodium and potash be kept in a *contiguous* position on the shelf."

"Gentleman to three-fourteen," said the clerk, hastily. I was whisked away to my room.

The next day I bought a trunk and clothing, and began to live the life of Edward Pinkhammer. I did not tax my brain with endeavours to solve problems of the past.

It was a piquant and sparkling cup that the great island city held up to my lips. I drank of it gratefully. The keys of Manhattan belong to him who is able to bear them. You must be either the city's guest or its victim.

The following few days were as gold and silver. Edward Pinkhammer, yet counting back to his birth by hours only, knew the rare joy of having come upon so diverting a world full-fledged and unrestrained. I sat entranced on the magic carpets provided in theatres and roof-gardens, that transported one into strange and delightful lands full of frolicsome music, pretty girls and *grotesque drolly extravagant parodies* upon human kind.

Auriferous - *Yielding*
Grotesque - *Odd/ unnatural in shape*
Drolly - *Amusing in an odd way*
Parodies - *Mimicries*
Spectacular - *Breath taking*

I went here and there at my own dear will, bound by no limits of space, time or comportment. I dined in weird cabarets, at weirder *tables d'hote* to the sound of Hungarian music and the wild shouts of mercurial artists and sculptors. Or, again, where the night life quivers in the electric glare like a *kinetoscopic* picture, and the millinery of the world, and its jewels, and the ones whom they adorn, and the men who make all three possible are met for good cheer and the *spectacular* effect.

And among all these scenes that I have mentioned I learned one thing that I never knew before. And that is that the key to liberty is not in the hands of License, but Convention holds it. Comity has a toll-gate at which you must pay, or you may not enter the land of Freedom. In all the glitter, the seeming disorder, the parade, the abandon, I saw this law, *unobtrusive*, yet like iron, prevail. Therefore, in Manhattan you must obey these unwritten laws, and then you will be freest of the free. If you decline to be bound by them, you put on shackles.

Sometimes, as my mood urged me, I would seek the stately, softly murmuring palm rooms, redolent with high-born life and delicate restraint, in which to dine. Again I would go down to the waterways in steamers packed with *vociferous*, *bedecked*, unchecked love-making clerks and shop-girls to their crude pleasures on the island shores. And there was always Broadway - glistening, opulent, wily, varying, desirable Broadway - growing upon one like an opium habit.

One afternoon as I entered my hotel a stout man with a big nose and a black moustache blocked my way in the corridor. When I would have passed around him, he greet me with offensive familiarity.

"Hello, Bellford!" he cried, loudly. "What the deuce are you doing in New York? Didn't know anything could drag you away from that old book den of yours. Is Mrs. B. along or is this a little business run alone, eh?"

"You have made a mistake, sir," I said, coldly, releasing my hand from his grasp. "My name is Pinkhammer. You will excuse me."

Unobtrusive - *Not noticeable*
Vociferous - *Crying out noisily*
Bedecked - *Adorned, decorated*
Apparently - *Visible clearly*

The man dropped to one side, *apparently* astonished. As I walked to the clerk's desk I heard him call to a bell boy and say something about telegraph blanks.

"You will give me my bill," I said to the clerk, "and have my baggage brought down in half an hour. I do not care to remain where I am annoyed by confidence men."

I moved that afternoon to another hotel, a sedate, old-fashioned one on lower Fifth Avenue.

There was a restaurant a little way off Broadway where one could be served almost *al fresco* in a tropic array of screening flora. Quiet and luxury and a perfect service made it an ideal place in which to take luncheon or refreshment. One afternoon I was there picking my way to a table among the ferns when I felt my sleeve caught.

"Mr. Bellford!" exclaimed an amazingly sweet voice.

I turned quickly to see a lady seated alone - a lady of about thirty, with exceedingly handsome eyes, who looked at me as though I had been her very dear friend.

"You were about to pass me," she said, accusingly. "Don't tell me you do not know me. Why should we not shake hands - at least once in fifteen years?"

I shook hands with her at once. I took a chair opposite her at the table. I summoned with my eyebrows a *hovering* waiter. The lady was *philandering* with an orange ice. I ordered a *creme de menthe*. Her hair was reddish bronze. You could not look at it, because you could not look away from her eyes. But you were conscious of it as you are conscious of sunset while you look into the *profundities* of a wood at twilight.

"Are you sure you know me?" I asked.

"No," she said, smiling. "I was never sure of that."

"What would you think," I said, a little anxiously, "if I were to tell you that my name is Edward Pinkhammer, from Cornopolis, Kansas?"

"What would I think?" she repeated, with a merry glance. "Why, that you had not brought Mrs. Bellford to New York with you, of course. I do wish you had. I would have liked to see Marian." Her voice lowered slightly - "You haven't changed much, Elwyn."

Hovering - *Lingering about*
Philandering - *Flirting*
Flouted - *To show contempts*
Timorously - *Fearful*

I felt her wonderful eyes searching mine and my face more closely.

"Yes, you have," she amended, and there was a soft, exultant note in her latest tones; "I see it now. You haven't forgotten. You haven't forgotten for a year or a day or an hour. I told you you never could."

I poked my straw anxiously in the *creme de menthe*.

"I'm sure I beg your pardon," I said, a little uneasy at her gaze. "But that is just the trouble. I have forgotten. I've forgotten everything."

She *flouted* my denial. She laughed deliciously at something she seemed to see in my face.

"I've heard of you at times," she went on. "You're quite a big lawyer out West - Denver, isn't it, or Los Angeles? Marian must be very proud of you. You knew, I suppose, that I married six months after you did. You may have seen it in the papers. The flowers alone cost two thousand dollars."

She had mentioned fifteen years. Fifteen years is a long time.

"Would it be too late," I asked, somewhat timorously, "to offer you congratulations?"

"Not if you dare do it," she answered, with such fine *intrepidity* that I was silent, and began to crease patterns on the cloth with my thumb nail.

"Tell me one thing," she said, leaning toward me rather eagerly - "a thing I have wanted to know for many years - just from a woman's curiosity, of course - have you ever dared since that night to touch, smell or look at white roses - at white roses wet with rain and dew?"

I took a sip of *creme de menthe*.

"It would be useless, I suppose," I said, with a sigh, "for me to repeat that I have no recollection at all about these things. My memory is completely at fault. I need not say how much I regret it."

The lady rested her arms upon the table, and again her eyes *disdained* my words and went traveling by their own route direct to my soul. She laughed softly, with a strange quality in the sound - it was a laugh of happiness - yes, and of content - and of misery. I tried to look away from her.

Intrepidity -
Disdained -
Concede -
Delegates -

"You lie, Elwyn Bellford," she breathed, blissfully. "Oh, I know you lie!"

I gazed dully into the ferns.

"My name is Edward Pinkhammer," I said. "I came with the **delegates** to the Druggists' National Convention. There is a movement on foot for arranging a new position for the bottles of tartrate of antimony and tartrate of potash, in which, very likely, you would take little interest."

A shining landau stopped before the entrance. The lady rose. I took her hand, and bowed.

"I am deeply sorry," I said to her, "that I cannot remember. I could explain, but fear you would not understand. You will not concede Pinkhammer; and I really cannot at all conceive of the - the roses and other things."

"Good-by, Mr. Bellford," she said, with her happy, sorrowful smile, as she stepped into her carriage.

I attended the theatre that night. When I returned to my hotel, a quiet man in dark clothes, who seemed interested in rubbing his finger nails with a silk handkerchief, appeared, magically, at my side.

"Mr. Pinkhammer," he said, giving the bulk of his attention to his forefinger, "may I request you to step aside with me for a little conversation? There is a room here."

"Certainly," I answered.

He conducted me into a small, private parlour. A lady and a gentleman were there. The lady, I surmised, would have been unusually good-looking had her features not been clouded by an expression of keen worry and fatigue. She was of a style of figure and possessed colouring and features that were agreeable to my fancy. She was in a travelling dress; she fixed upon me an earnest look of extreme **anxiety**, and pressed an unsteady hand to her bosom. I think she would have started forward, but the gentleman arrested her movement with an authoritative motion of his hand. He then came, himself, to meet me. He was a man of forty, a little grey about the temples, and with a strong, thoughtful face.

"Bellford, old man," he said, cordially, "I'm glad to see you again. Of course we know everything is all right. I warned you,

Wearisome - *Tiresome*
Wailing - *Crying loudly*
Detaining - *To keep under restraint*
Allusion - *A passing*
Moaned - *Sound of pain*

you know, that you were overdoing it. Now, you'll go back with us, and be yourself again in no time."

I smiled ironically.

"I have been 'Bellforded' so often," I said, "that it has lost its edge. Still, in the end, it may grow wearisome. Would you be willing at all to entertain the hypothesis that my name is Edward Pinkhammer, and that I never saw you before in my life?"

Before the man could reply a wailing cry came from the woman. She sprang past his detaining arm. "Elwyn!" she sobbed, and cast herself upon me, and clung tight. "Elwyn," she cried again, "don't break my heart. I am your wife - call my name once - just once. I could see you dead rather than this way."

I unwound her arms respectfully, but firmly.

"Madam," I said, severely, "pardon me if I suggest that you accept a resemblance too precipitately. It is a pity," I went on, with an amused laugh, as the thought occurred to me, "that this Bellford and I could not be kept side by side upon the same shelf like tartrates of sodium and antimony for purposes of identification. In order to understand the allusion," I concluded airily, "it may be necessary for you to keep an eye on the proceedings of the Druggists' National Convention."

The lady turned to her companion, and grasped his arm.

"What is it, Doctor Volney? Oh, what is it?" she moaned.

"Go to your room for a while," I heard him say. "I will remain and talk with him. His mind? No, I think not - only a portion of the brain. Yes, I am sure he will recover. Go to your room and leave me with him."

The lady disappeared. The man in dark clothes also went outside, still *manicuring* himself in a thoughtful way. I think he waited in the hall.

"I would like to talk with you a while, Mr. Pinkhammer, if I may," said the gentleman who remained.

"Very well, if you care to," I replied, "and will excuse me if I take it comfortably; I am rather tired." I stretched myself upon a *couch* by a window and lit a cigar. He drew a chair nearby.

"Let us speak to the point," he said, *soothingly*. "Your name is not Pinkhammer."

Manicuring - A *cosmetic treatment of the hands*
Couch - A *bed*
Soothingly - *Calminghy*
Extravagantly - *Spending more than necessary*
Christens - *To give name to at baptism*

"I know that as well as you do," I said, coolly. "But a man must have a name of some sort. I can assure you that I do not **extravagantly** admire the name of Pinkhammer. But when one christens one's self suddenly, the fine names do not seem to suggest themselves. But, suppose it had been Scheringhausen or Scroggins! I think I did very well with Pinkhammer."

"Your name," said the other man, seriously, "is Elwyn C. Bellford. You are one of the first lawyers in Denver. You are suffering from an attack of aphasia, which has caused you to forget your identity. The cause of it was over-application to your profession, and, perhaps, a life too bare of natural recreation and pleasures. The lady who has just left the room is your wife."

"She is what I would call a fine-looking woman," I said, after a judicial pause. "I particularly admire the shade of brown in her hair."

"She is a wife to be proud of. Since your disappearance, nearly two weeks ago, she has scarcely closed her eyes. We learned that you were in New York through a telegram sent by Isidore Newman, a traveling man from Denver. He said that he had met you in a hotel here, and that you did not recognise him."

"I think I remember the occasion," I said. "The fellow called me 'Bellford,' if I am not mistaken. But don't you think it about time, now, for you to introduce yourself?"

"I am Robert Volney - Doctor Volney. I have been your close friend for twenty years, and your physician for fifteen. I came with Mrs. Bellford to trace you as soon as we got the telegram. Try, Elwyn, old man - try to remember!"

"What's the use to try?" I asked, with a little frown. "You say you are a physician. Is aphasia curable? When a man loses his memory does it return slowly, or suddenly?"

"Sometimes gradually and imperfectly; sometimes as suddenly as it went."

"Will you undertake the treatment of my case, Doctor Volney?" I asked.

"Old friend," said he, "I'll do everything in my power, and will have done everything that science can do to cure you."

"Very well," said I. "Then you will consider that I am your patient. Everything is in confidence now - professional confidence."

Frown - *To contract the brow*

Sprinkled - *Scattered in drops*

Fragrant - *Having a pleasant*

Shin - *The front part of the leg*

"Of course," said Doctor Volney.

I got up from the couch. Some one had set a vase of white roses on the centre table - a cluster of white roses, freshly sprinkled and fragrant. I threw them far out of the window, and then laid myself upon the couch again.

"It will be best, Bobby," I said, "to have this cure happen suddenly. I'm rather tired of it all, anyway. You may go now and bring Marian in. But, oh, Doc," I said, with a sigh, as I kicked him on the shin - "good old Doc - it was glorious!"

Food For Thought

" I got up from the couch. Somone had set a vase of white roses on the centre table - I threw them far out of the window , and then laid myself upon the couch again." Do you think the bun ch of white roses brought back Belford's memory, or Belford never had any attack of Aphasis, he just was tired and sick of his routine life wanting some change. Support your answer with relevant reasons.

Best Stories of O.Henry

A Night In New Arabia

THe great city of Bagdad-on-the-Subway is caliph-ridden. Its palaces, bazaars, khans, and byways are thronged with Al Rashids in divers disguises, seeking diversion and victims for their unbridled generosity. You can scarcely find a poor beggar whom they are willing to let enjoy his spoils *unsuccored*, nor a *wrecked* unfortunate upon whom they will not reshower the means of fresh misfortune. You will hardly find anywhere a hungry one who has not had the opportunity to tighten his belt in gift libraries, nor a poor pundit who has not blushed at the holiday basket of celery-crowned turkey forced *resoundingly* through his door by the *eleemosynary* press.

So then, fearfully through the Harun-haunted streets creep the one-eyed calenders, the Little Hunchback and the Barber's Sixth Brother, hoping to escape the ministrations of the roving *horde* of *caliphoid* sultans.

Entertainment for many Arabian nights might be had from the histories of those who have escaped the largesse of the army of Commanders of the Faithful. Until dawn you might sit on the enchanted rug and listen to such stories as are told of the powerful genie Roc-Ef-El-Er who sent the Forty Thieves to soak up the oil plant of Ali Baba; of the good Caliph Kar-Neg-Ghe, who gave away palaces; of the Seven Voyages of Sailbad, the Sinner, who frequented wooden excursion steamers among the islands; of the Fisherman and the Bottle; of the Barmecides' Boarding house; of Aladdin's rise to wealth by means of his Wonderful Gasmeter.

But now, there being ten sultans to one Sheherazade, she is held too valuable to be in fear of the bowstring. In consequence the art of narrative languishes. And, as the lesser caliphs are hunting the happy poor and the resigned unfortunate from cover to cover in order to heap upon them strange mercies and mysterious benefits, too often comes the report from Arabian headquarters that the captive refused "to talk."

This reticence, then, in the actors who perform the sad comedies of their philanthropy-scourged world, must, in a

Unsuccored - *Without help*
Wrecked - *Reduce a slate run*
Resoundingly - *Uttered loudly*
Eleemosynary - *Derived from*
Harun - *Haunted*
Horde - *A tribe*

degree, account for the shortcomings of this painfully gleaned tale, which shall be called: THE STORY OF THE CALIPH WHO *ALLEVIATED* HIS CONSCIENCE

Old Jacob Spraggins mixed for himself some Scotch and lithia water at his $1,200 oak sideboard. Inspiration must have resulted from its *imbibition,* for immediately afterward he struck the quartered oak soundly with his fist and shouted to the empty dining room:

"By the coke ovens of hell, it must be that ten thousand dollars! If I can get that squared, it'll do the trick."

Thus, by the commonest *artifice* of the trade, having gained your interest, the action of the story will now be suspended, leaving you *grumpily* to consider a sort of dull biography beginning fifteen years before.

When old Jacob was young Jacob he was a breaker boy in a Pennsylvania coal mine. I don't know what a breaker boy is; but his occupation seems to be standing by a coal dump with a wan look and a dinner-pail to have his picture taken for magazine articles. Anyhow, Jacob was one. But, instead of dying of overwork at nine, and leaving his helpless parents and brothers at the mercy of the union strikers' reserve fund, he hitched up his *galluses,* put a dollar or two in a side proposition now and then, and at forty-five was worth $20,000,000.

There now! it's over. Hardly had time to *yawn,* did you? I've seen biographies that - but let us *dissemble.*

I want you to consider Jacob Spraggins, Esq., after he had arrived at the seventh stage of his career. The stages meant are, first, humble origin; second, deserved promotion; third, stockholder; fourth, capitalist; fifth, trust magnate; sixth, rich malefactor; seventh, caliph; eighth, x. The eighth stage shall be left to the higher mathematics.

At fifty-five Jacob retired from active business. The income of a czar was still rolling in on him from coal, iron, real estate, oil, railroads, manufactories, and corporations, but none of it touched Jacob's hands in a raw state. It was a *sterilized increment,* carefully cleaned and dusted and fumigated until it arrived at its ultimate stage of untainted, spotless checks in the white fingers of his private secretary. Jacob built a three-million-dollar palace on a corner lot fronting

Aleviated - *Raised*
Imbibition - *The absorption of solvent by a get*
Artifice - *A clever trick*
Grumpily - *Discontentedly*
Dissemble - *To open wide like a mouth*
Increment - *Something added*

on Nabob Avenue, city of New Bagdad, and began to feel the mantle of the late H. A. Rashid descending upon him. Eventually, Jacob slipped the mantle under his collar, tied it in a neat four-in-hand, and became a licensed *harrier* of our Mesopotamian *proletariat*.

When a man's income becomes so large that the butcher actually sends him the kind of steak he orders, he begins to think about his soul's salvation. Now, the various stages or classes of rich men must not be forgotten. The capitalist can tell you to a dollar the amount of his wealth. The trust *magnate* "estimates" it. The rich malefactor hands you a cigar and denies that he has bought the P. D. & Q. The caliph merely smiles and talks about Hammerstein and the musical *lasses*.

There is a record of tremendous altercation at breakfast in a "Where-to-Dine-Well" tavern between a magnate and his wife, the rift within the loot being that the wife calculated their fortune at a figure $3,000,000 higher than did her future *divorce*. Oh, well, I, myself, heard a similar quarrel between a man and his wife because he found fifty cents less in his pockets than he thought he had. After all, we are all human - Count Tolstoi, R. Fitzsimmons, Peter Pan, and the rest of us.

Don't lose heart because the story seems to be *degenerating* into a sort of moral essay for intellectual readers.

There will be dialogue and stage business pretty soon.

When Jacob first began to compare the eyes of needles with the camels in the Zoo he decided upon organized charity. He had his secretary send a check for one million to the Universal Benevolent Association of the Globe. You may have looked down through a *grating* in front of a decayed warehouse for a nickel that you had dropped through. But that is neither here nor there. The Association acknowledged receipt of his favor of the 24th ult. with enclosure as stated.

Separated by a double line, but still mighty close to the matter under the caption of "Oddities of the Day's News" in an evening paper, Jacob Spraggins read that one "Jasper Spargyous" had "donated $100,000 to the U. B. A. of G." A camel may have a stomach for each day in the week; but I dare not *venture* to accord him whiskers, for fear of the Great Displeasure at Washington; but if he have whiskers, surely not one of them will seem to have been inserted in the

Harrier - *Medium-sized hounds*
Proletariat - *A class of wage earners*
Magnate - *A person of great influence*
Lasses - *Young women*
Degenerating - *Decaying*
Grating - *Imitating*
Venture - *Furnished with*

eye of a needle by that effort of that rich man to enter the K. of H. The right is reserved to reject any and all bids; signed, S. Peter, secretary and gatekeeper.

Next, Jacob selected the best *endowed* college he could scare up and presented it with a $200,000 laboratory. The college did not maintain a scientific course, but it accepted the money and built an elaborate *lavatory* instead, which was no *diversion* of funds so far as Jacob ever discovered.

The faculty met and invited Jacob to come over and take his A B C degree. Before sending the invitation they smiled, cut out the C, added the proper punctuation marks, and all was well.

While walking on the campus before being capped and *gowned*, Jacob saw two professors strolling nearby. Their voices, long adapted to indoor *acoustics*, undesignedly reached his ear.

"There goes the latest *chevalier d'industrie*," said one of them, "to buy a sleeping powder from us. He gets his degree to-morrow."

"*In foro conscientai*," said the other. "Let's 'eave 'arf a brick at 'im."

Jacob ignored the Latin, but the brick pleasantry was not too hard for him. There was no *mandragora* in the honourary draught of learning that he had bought. That was before the passage of the Pure Food and Drugs Act.

Jacob wearied of philanthropy on a large scale.

"If I could see folks made happier," he said to himself - "If I could see 'em myself and hear 'em express their gratitude for what I done for 'em it would make me feel better. This donatin' funds to institutions and societies is about as satisfactory as dropping money into a broken slot machine."

So Jacob followed his nose, which led him through unswept streets to the homes of the poorest. "The very thing!" said Jacob. "I will charter two river steamboats, pack them full of these unfortunate children and - say ten thousand dolls and drums and a thousand freezers of ice cream, and give them a delightful outing up the Sound. The sea breezes on that trip ought to blow the *taint* off some of this money that keeps coming in faster than I can work it off my mind."

Lavatory - *A flush toilet*
Gowned - *To dress in a gown*
Acoustics - *Related to the sense of hearing*
Mandragora - *A eurasian plant*
Taint - *A trade fo something too*

Jacob must have leaked some of his *benevolent intentions*, for an immense person with a bald face and a mouth that looked as if it ought to have a "Drop Letters Here" sign over it hooked a finger around him and set him in a space between a barber's pole and a stack of ash cans. Words came out of the post-office slit - smooth, husky words with gloves on 'em, but sounding as if they might turn to bare knuckles any moment.

"Say, Sport, do you know where you are at? Well, dis is Mike O'Grady's district you're buttin' into - see? Mike's got de stomach-ache privilege for every kid in dis neighbourhood - see? And if dere's any picnics or red balloons to be dealt out here, Mike's money pays for 'em - see? Don't you butt in, or something'll be handed to you. Youse d - - settlers and reformers with your *social ologies* and your millionaire detectives have got dis district in a hell of a fix, anyhow. With your college students and professors rough-housing de soda-water stands and dem rubber-neck coaches fillin' de streets, de folks down here are 'fraid to go out of de houses. Now, you leave 'em to Mike. Dey belongs to him, and he knows how to handle 'em. Keep on your own side of de town. Are you some wiser now, uncle, or do you want to scrap wit' Mike O'Grady for de Santa Claus belt in dis district?"

Clearly, that spot in the moral vineyard was *preempted*. So Caliph Spraggins menaced no more the people in the bazaars of the East Side. To keep down his growing surplus he doubled his donations to organised charity, presented the Y. M. C. A. of his native town with a $10,000 collection of butterflies, and sent a check to the famine sufferers in China big enough to buy new emerald eyes and diamond-filled teeth for all their gods. But none of these charitable acts seemed to bring peace to the caliph's heart.

He tried to get a personal note into his *benefactions* by tipping bellboys and waiters $10 and $20 bills. He got well snickered at and derided for that by the minions who accept with respect gratuities *commensurate* to the service performed. He sought out an ambitious and talented but poor young woman, and bought for her the star part in a new comedy. He might have gotten rid of $50,000 more of his *cumbersome* money in this philanthropy if he had not neglected to

Preempted - *To acquire before someone else*
Benefaction - *The act of doing good*
Commensurate - *Proportionate, adequate*
Cumbersome - *Troublesome*

Best Stories of O.Henry

write letters to her. But she lost the suit for lack of evidence, while his capital still kept piling up, and his *optikos needleorum camelibus* - or rich man's disease - was unrelieved.

In Caliph Spraggins's $3,000,000 home lived his sister Henrietta, who used to cook for the coal miners in a twenty-five-cent eating house in Coketown, Pa., and who now would have offered John Mitchell only two fingers of her hand to shake. And his daughter Celia, nineteen, back from boarding-school and from being polished off by private instructors in the restaurant languages and those 'etudes and things.

Celia is the heroine. Lest the artist's **delineation** of her charms on this very page humbug your fancy, take from me her authorised description. She was a nice-looking, awkward, loud, rather bashful, brown-haired girl, with a sallow complexion, bright eyes, and a perpetual smile. She had a wholesome, Spraggins-inherited love for plain food, loose clothing, and the society of the lower classes. She had too much health and youth to feel the burden of wealth. She had a wide mouth that kept the peppermint-pepsin tablets rattling like hail from the slot-machine wherever she went, and she could whistle hornpipes. Keep this picture in mind; and let the artist do his worst.

Celia looked out of her window one day and gave her heart to the **grocer's** young man. The receiver thereof was at that moment engaged in conceding **immortality** to his horse and calling down upon him the ultimate fate of the wicked; so he did not notice the transfer. A horse should stand still when you are lifting a crate of strictly new-laid eggs out of the wagon.

Young lady reader, you would have liked that grocer's young man yourself. But you wouldn't have given him your heart, because you are saving it for a riding-master, or a shoe-manufacturer with a torpid liver, or something quiet but rich in gray tweeds at Palm Beach. Oh, I know about it. So I am glad the grocer's young man was for Celia, and not for you.

The grocer's young man was slim and straight and as confident and easy in his movements as the man in the back of the magazines who wears the new frictionless roller suspenders. He wore a gray bicycle cap on the back of his head, and his hair was straw-coloured and curly, and his

Delineation -
Description
Everlasting - *Forever*
Wagon - *Four-wheeled*
Contemptuous -
Sneering

sunburned face looked like one that smiled a good deal when he was not preaching the doctrine of *everlasting* punishment to delivery-wagon horses. He slung imported A1 fancy groceries about as though they were only the stuff he delivered at boarding-houses; and when he picked up his whip, your mind instantly recalled Mr. Tacktt and his air with the buttonless foils.

Tradesmen delivered their goods at a side gate at the rear of the house. The grocer's *wagon* came about ten in the morning. For three days Celia watched the driver when he came, finding something new each time to admire in the lofty and almost *contemptuous* way he had of tossing around the choicest gifts of Pomona, Ceres, and the *canning* factories. Then she consulted Annette.

To be *explicit*, Annette McCorkle, the second housemaid who deserves a paragraph herself. Annette Fletcherized large numbers of romantic novels which she obtained at a free public library branch (donated by one of the biggest caliphs in the business). She was Celia's sidekicker and chum, though Aunt Henrietta didn't know it, you may hazard a bean or two.

"Oh, canary-bird seed!" exclaimed Annette. "Ain't it a corkin' situation? You a heiress, and fallin' in love with him on sight! He's a sweet boy, too, and above his business. But he ain't *susceptible* like the common run of grocer's assistants. He never pays no attention to me."

"He will to me," said Celia.

"Riches -" began Annette, unsheathing the not unjustifiable feminine sting.

"Oh, you're not so beautiful," said Celia, with her wide, *disarming* smile. "Neither am I; but he sha'n't know that there's any money mixed up with my looks, such as they are. That's fair. Now, I want you to lend me one of your caps and an apron, Annette."

"Oh, marshmallows!" cried Annette. "I see. Ain't it lovely? It's just like 'Lurline, the Left-Handed; or, A Buttonhole Maker's Wrongs.' I'll bet he'll turn out to be a count."

There was a long hallway (or "passageway," as they call it in the land of the Colonels) with one side latticed, running along the rear of the house. The grocer's young man went through this to deliver his goods. One morning he passed a

Canning - The act or process of preserving cooked food
Explicit - Clearly develped
Susceptible - Capable of being affected
Disarming - Winsome, engaging
Cumbered - Hindered
Piccolos - A small flute

girl in there with shining eyes, sallow complexion, and wide, smiling mouth, wearing a maid's cap and apron. But as he was *cumbered* with a basket of Early Drumhead lettuce and Trophy tomatoes and three bunches of asparagus and six bottles of the most expensive Queen olives, he saw no more than that she was one of the maids.

But on his way out he came up behind her, and she was whistling "Fisher's Hornpipe" so loudly and clearly that all the *piccolos* in the world should have *disjointed* themselves and crept into their cases for shame.

The grocer's young man stopped and pushed back his cap until it hung on his collar button behind.

"That's out o' sight, Kid," said he.

"My name is Celia, if you please," said the *whistler*, dazzling him with a three-inch smile.

That's all right. I'm Thomas McLeod. What part of the house do you work in?"

"I'm the - the second parlor maid."

"Do you know the 'Falling Waters'?"

"No," said Celia, "we don't know anybody. We got rich too quick - that is, Mr. Spraggins did." "I'll make you *acquainted*," said Thomas McLeod. "It's a strathspey - the first cousin to a hornpipe." If Celia's whistling put the piccolos out of commission, Thomas McLeod's surely made the biggest flutes hunt their holes. He could actually whistle *bass*.

When he stopped Celia was ready to jump into his delivery wagon and ride with him clear to the end of the pier and on to the ferry-boat of the Charon line.

"I'll be around to-morrow at 10:15," said Thomas, "with some spinach and a case of carbonic." "I'll practice that what-you-may-call-it," said Celia. "I can whistle a fine second."

The processes of courtship are personal, and do not belong to general literature. They should be chronicled in detail only in advertisements of iron tonics and in the secret by-laws of the Woman's Auxiliary of the Ancient Order of the Rat Trap. But *genteel* writing may contain a description of certain stages of its progress without intruding upon the province of the X-ray or of park policemen.

Whistler - *A person thing*
Acquainted - *Familar refined*
Genteel - *Well-breet*
Latticed - *Furnished*
Invincible - *Incapable of being conquered defeated*

A day came when Thomas McLeod and Celia lingered at the end of the *latticed* "passage." "Sixteen a week isn't much," said Thomas, letting his cap rest on his shoulder blades.

Celia looked through the lattice-work and whistled a dead march. Shopping with Aunt Henrietta the day before, she had paid that much for a dozen handkerchiefs.

"Maybe I'll get a raise next month," said Thomas. "I'll be around to-morrow at the same time with a bag of flour and the laundry soap."

"All right," said Celia. "Annette's married cousin pays only $20 a month for a flat in the Bronx." Never for a moment did she count on the Spraggins money. She knew Aunt Henrietta's *invincible* pride of caste and pa's mightiness as a Colossus of cash, and she understood that if she chose Thomas she and her grocer's young man might go whistle for a living.

Another day came, Thomas violating the dignity of Nabob Avenue with "The Devil's Dream," whistled keenly between his teeth.

"Raised to eighteen a week yesterday," he said. "Been pricing flats around Morningside. You want to start untying those *apron* strings and *unpinning* that cap, old girl."

"Oh, Tommy!" said Celia, with her broadest smile. "Won't that be enough? I got Betty to show me how to make a cottage pudding. I guess we could call it a flat *pudding* if we wanted to."

"And tell no lie," said Thomas.

"And I can sweep and polish and dust - of course, a parlour maid learns that. And we cold whistle duets of evenings."

"The old man said he'd raise me to twenty at Christmas if Bryan couldn't think of any harder name to call a Republican than a '*postponer*,'" said the grocer's young man.

"I can sew," said Celia; "and I know that you must make the gas company's man show his badge when he comes to look at the meter; and I know how to put up *quince* jam and window curtains."

"Bully! you're all right, Cele. Yes, I believe we can pull it off on eighteen."

Unpinning - *To remove pins from*
Pudding - *A thick, soft dessert*
Postponer - *To put off to a later time*
Quince - *A small widely cultivated Asian rosaceous tree*

As he was jumping into the wagon the second parlor maid braved discovery by running swiftly to the gate.

"And, oh, Tommy, I forgot," she called, softly. "I believe I could make your neckties."

"Forget it," said Thomas decisively.

"And another thing," she continued. "Sliced cucumbers at night will drive away cockroaches." "And sleep, too, you bet," said Mr. McLeod. "Yes, I believe if I have a delivery to make on the West Side this afternoon I'll look in at a furniture store I know over there."

It was just as the wagon dashed away that old Jacob Spraggins struck the sideboard with his fist and made the mysterious remark about ten thousand dollars that you perhaps remember. Which justifies the reflection that some stories, as well as life, and puppies thrown into wells, move around in circles. Painfully but briefly we must shed light on Jacob's words.

The foundation of his fortune was made when he was twenty. A poor coal-digger (ever hear of a rich one?) had saved a dollar or two and bought a small tract of land on a hillside on which he tried to raise corn. Not a *nubbin*. Jacob, whose nose was a divining-rod, told him there was a vein of coal beneath. he bought the land from the miner for $125 and sold it a month afterward for $10,000. Luckily the miner had enough left of his sale money to drink himself into a black coat opening in the back, as soon as he heard the news.

And so, for forty years afterward, we find Jacob illuminated with the sudden thought that if he could make restitution of this sum of money to the heirs or assigns of the unlucky miner, *respite* and Nepenthe might be his.

And now must come swift action, for we have here some four thousand words and not a tear shed and never a pistol, joke, safe, nor bottle cracked.

Old Jacob hired a dozen private detectives to find the heirs, if any existed, of the old miner, Hugh McLeod.

Get the point? Of course I know as well as you do that Thomas is going to be the heir. I might have concealed the name; but why always hold back you mystery till the end?

Nubbin - *A small lump*

Respite - *Temporary relief*

Restitution - *Restoration of property*

I say, let it come near the middle so people can stop reading there if they want to.

After the detectives had trailed false clues about three thousand dollars - I mean miles - they cornered Thomas at the grocery and got his confession that Hugh McLeod had been his grandfather, and that there were no other heirs. They arranged a meeting for him and old Jacob one morning in one of their offices.

Jacob liked the young man very much. He liked the way he looked straight at him when he talked, and the way he threw his bicycle cap over the top of a rose-colored vase on the centre-table. There was a slight flaw in Jacob's system of *restitution*. He did not consider that the act, to be perfect, should include confession. So he represented himself to be the agent of the purchaser of the land who had sent him to refund the sale price for the ease of his conscience.

"Well, sir," said Thomas, "this sounds to me like an illustrated post-card from South Boston with 'We're having a good time here' written on it. I don't know the game. Is this ten thousand dollars money, or do I have to save so many coupons to get it?"

Old Jacob counted out to him twenty five-hundred-dollar bills.

That was better, he thought, than a check. Thomas put them thoughtfully into his pocket.

"Grandfather's best thanks," he said, "to the party who sends it."

Jacob talked on, asking him about his work, how he spent his *leisure* time, and what his ambitions were. The more he saw and heard of Thomas, the better he liked him. He had not met many young men in Bagdad so frank and wholesome.

"I would like to have you visit my house," he said. "I might help you in *investing* or laying out your money. I am a very wealthy man. I have a daughter about grown, and I would like for you to know her. There are not many young men I would care to have call on her."

Leisure - *Free or unoccupied*
Estate - *A piece of landed property*
Investing - *To put money to use, by purchase*

"I'm obliged," said Thomas. "I'm not much at making calls. It's generally the side entrance for mine. And, besides, I'm engaged to a girl that has the Delaware peach crop killed in the blossom. She's a parlor maid in a house where I deliver goods. She won't be working there much longer, though. Say, don't forget to give your friend my grandfather's best regards. You'll excuse me now; my wagon's outside with a lot of green stuff that's got to be delivered. See you again, sir."

At eleven Thomas delivered some bunches of parsley and lettuce at the Spraggins mansion. Thomas was only twenty-two; so, as he came back, he took out the handful of five-hundred-dollar bills and waved them carelessly. Annette took a pair of eyes as big as creamed onion to the cook.

"I told you he was a count," she said, after relating. "He never would carry on with me."

"But you say he showed money," said the cook.

"Hundreds of thousands," said Annette. "Carried around loose in his pockets. And he never would look at me."

"It was paid to me to-day," Thomas was explaining to Celia outside. "It came from my grandfather's *estate*. Say, Cele, what's the use of waiting now? I'm going to quit the job to-night. Why can't we get married next week?"

"Tommy," said Celia. "I'm no parlor maid. I've been fooling you. I'm Miss Spraggins - Celia Spraggins. The newspapers say I'll be worth forty million dollars some day."

Thomas pulled his cap down straight on his head for the first time since we have known him. "I suppose then," said he, "I suppose then you'll not be marrying me next week. But you *can* whistle."

"No," said Celia, "I'll not be marrying you next week. My father would never let me marry a grocer's clerk. But I'll marry you to-night, Tommy, if you say so."

Old Jacob Spraggins came home at 9:30 P. M., in his motor car. The make of it you will have to surmise sorrowfully; I am giving you *unsubsidized* fiction; had it been a street car I could have told you its *voltage* and the number of wheels it had. Jacob called for his daughter; he had bought a ruby necklace for her, and wanted to hear her say what a kind, thoughtful, dear old dad he was.

Voltage - *An electromotive force/ potential difference expressed in volts*
Unsubsidized - *No aids*
Remorseful - *Regretful*
Histrionics - *Dramatic representations*

There was a brief search in the house for her, and then came Annette, glowing with the pure flame of truth and loyalty well mixed with envy and *histrionics*.

"Oh, sir," said she, wondering if she should kneel, "Miss Celia's just this minute running away out of the side gate with a young man to be married. I couldn't stop her, sir. They went in a cab."

"What young man?" roared old Jacob.

"A millionaire, if you please, sir - a rich nobleman in disguise. He carries his money with him, and the red peppers and the onions was only to blind us, sir. He never did seem to take to me."

Jacob rushed out in time to catch his car. The chauffeur had been delayed by trying to light a cigarette in the wind.

"Here, Gaston, or Mike, or whatever you call yourself, scoot around the corner quicker than *blazes* and see if you can see a cab. If you do, run it down."

There was a cab in sight a block away. Gaston, or Mike, with his eyes half shut and his mind on his cigarette, picked up the trail, neatly crowded the cab to the curb and pocketed it. "What t'ell you doin'?" yelled the cabman.

"Pa!" shrieked Celia.

"Grandfather's *remorseful* friend's agent!" said Thomas. "Wonder what's on his conscience now."

"A thousand thunders," said Gaston, or Mike. "I have no other match."

"Young man," said old Jacob, severely, "how about that parlor maid you were engaged to?" A couple of years afterward old Jacob went into the office of his private secretary.

"The Amalgamated Missionary Society solicits a contribution of $30,000 toward the conversion of the Koreans," said the secretary.

"Pass 'em up," said Jacob.

"The University of Plumville writes that its yearly *endowment* fund of $50,000 that you bestowed upon it is past due."

"Tell 'em it's been cut out."

"The Scientific Society of Clam Cove, Long Island, asks for $10,000 to buy alcohol to preserve specimens."

"Waste basket."

"The Society for Providing Healthful Recreation for Working Girls wants $20,000 from you to lay out a golf course."

"Tell 'em to see an undertaker."

"Cut 'em all out," went on Jacob. "I've quit being a good thing. I need every dollar I can scrape or save. I want you to write to the directors of every company that I'm interested in and recommend a 10 per cent. cut in salaries. And say - I noticed half a cake of soap lying in a corner of the hall as I came in. I want you to speak to the *scrubwoman* about waste. I've got no money to throw away. And say - we've got vinegar pretty well in hand, haven't we?'

"The Globe Spice & Seasons Company," said secretary, "controls the market at present."

"Raise vinegar two cents a gallon. Notify all our branches."

Suddenly Jacob Spraggin's plump red face relaxed into a pulpy grin. He walked over to the secretary's desk and showed a small red mark on his thick forefinger.

"Bit it," he said, "darned if he didn't, and he ain't had the tooth three weeks - Jaky McLeod, my Celia's kid. He'll be worth a hundred millions by the time he's twenty-one if I can pile it up for him."

As he was leaving, old Jacob turned at the door, and said:

"Better make that *vinegar* raise three cents instead of two. I'll be back in an hour and sign the letters."

The true history of the Caliph Harun Al Rashid relates that toward, the end of his reign he wearied of *philanthropy*, and caused to be *beheaded* all his former favorites and companions of his "Arabian Nights" *rambles*. Happy are we in these days of enlightenment, when the only death warrant the caliphs can serve on us is in the form of a tradesman's bill.

Philanthropy - *The practice of performing charitable actions*
Vinegar - *A sour liquid consisting*
Beheaded - *To cut off the head of*
Rambles - *To wander in an aimless manner*
Warrant - *Authorization*

Food For Thought

Celia plans to elope with Tom Mcleod. Spraggins follows her and is happy that his daughter has chosen Tom Mcleod. What happens a year later ofter Celia's marriage? Why does the author say that Spraggins never really changed? What does he do to amass a fortune for his grandson? Do you think that wealthy people like Spraggins never change and are always after money? Give one example other than this story.

The Gold That Glittered

A story with a moral appended is like the bill of a mosquito. It bores you, and then injects a stinging drop to *irritate* your *conscience*. Therefore let us have the moral first and be done with it. All is not gold that *glitters*, but it is a wise child that keeps the stopper in his bottle of testing acid.

Where Broadway skirts the corner of the square presided over by George the Veracious is the Little Rialto. Here stand the actors of that quarter, and this is their *shibboleth*: "'Nit,' says I to Frohman, 'you can't touch me for a *kopeck* less than two-fifty per,' and out I walks."

Westward and southward from the Thespian *glare* are one or two streets where a Spanish-American colony has huddled for a little tropical warmth in the *nipping* North. The centre of life in this *precinct* is "El Refugio," a cafe and restaurant that caters to the volatile exiles from the South. Up from Chili, Bolivia, Colombia, the rolling republics of Central America and the ireful islands of the Western Indies flit the cloaked and sombreroed senores, who are scattered like burning lava by the political eruptions of their several countries.

Hither they come to lay counterplots, to bide their time, to solicit funds, to enlist filibusterers, to smuggle out arms and *ammunitions*, to play the game at long taw. In El Refugio, they find the atmosphere in which they thrive.

In the restaurant of El Refugio are served compounds delightful to the palate of the man from Capricorn or Cancer. Altruism must halt the story thus long. On, diner, weary of the *culinary subterfuges* of the Gallic chef, hie thee to El Refugio! There only will you find a fish - bluefish, shad or pompano from the Gulf - baked after the Spanish method. Tomatoes give it color, individuality and soul; chili colorado bestows upon it zest, originality and fervor; unknown herbs furnish *piquancy* and mystery, and - but its crowning glory deserves a new sentence. Around it, above it, beneath it, in its *vicinity* - but never in it - hovers an *ethereal* aura, an *effluvium* so rarefied and delicate that only the Society for Psychical Research could note its origin. Do not say that garlic is in the fish at El Refugio. It is not otherwise than as if the spirit of Garlic, flitting past, has *wafted*

Vicinity - *The area*
Effluvium - *A slight*
Piquancy - *Spicy, sharp*
Subterfuges - *Deception scheme*
Shibboleth - *A slogan*
Precinet - *Encloseed area*

one kiss that *lingers* in the *parsley-crowned* dish as haunting as those kisses in life, "by hopeless fancy feigned on lips that are for others." And then, when Conchito, the waiter, brings you a plate of brown frijoles and carafe of wine that has never stood still between Oporto and El Refugio - ah, Dios!

One day a Hamburg-American liner deposited upon Pier No. 55 Gen. Perrico Ximenes Villablanca Falcon, a passenger from Cartagena. The General was between a claybank and bay in complexion, had a 42-inch waist and stood 5 feet 4 with his Du Barry heels. He had the mustache of a shooting-gallery *proprietor*, he wore the full dress of a Texas congressman and had the important aspect of an uninstructed delegate.

Gen. Falcon had enough English under his hat to enable him to inquire his way to the street in which El Refugio stood. When he reached that neighbourhood he saw a sign before a respectable red-brick house that read, "Hotel Espanol." In the window was a card in Spanish, "Aqui se habla Espanol." The General entered, sure of a congenial port.

In the cozy office was Mrs. O'Brien, the proprietress. She had blond - oh, *unimpeachably* blond hair. For the rest she was amiability, and ran largely to inches around. Gen. Falcon brushed the floor with his broad-brimmed hat, and emitted a quantity of Spanish, the syllables sounding like firecrackers gently popping their way down the string of a bunch.

"Spanish or Dago?" asked Mrs. O'Brien, pleasantly.

"I am a Colombian, madam," said the General, proudly. "I speak the Spanish. The advisment in your window say the Spanish he is spoken here. How is that?"

"Well, you've been speaking it, ain't you?" said the madam. "I'm sure I can't."

At the Hotel Espanol General Falcon engaged rooms and established himself. At dusk he *sauntered* out upon the streets to view the wonders of this roaring city of the North. As he walked he thought of the wonderful golden hair of Mme. O'Brien. "It is here," said the General to himself, no doubt in his own language, "that one shall find the most beautiful *senoras* in the world. I have not in my Colombia viewed among our beauties one so fair. But no! It is not for the General Falcon to think of beauty. It is my country that claims my devotion." At the corner of Broadway and the Little Rialto the General became involved. The street cars *bewildered* him,

Sauntered - *To walk with a leisurely gait*
Unimpeachably - *Above suspicion*
Wafted - *To remain*

and the *fender* of one upset him against a pushcart laden with oranges. A cab driver missed him an inch with a hub, and poured barbarous execrations upon his head. He *scrambled* to the *sidewalk* and skipped again in terror when the whistle of a peanut-roaster puffed a hot scream in his ear. V'algame Dios! What devil's city is this?"

As the General fluttered out of the streamers of passers like a wounded snipe he was marked simultaneously as game by two hunters. One was "Bully" McGuire, whose system of sport required the use of a strong arm and the misuse of an eight-inch piece of lead pipe. The other Nimrod of the asphalt was "Spider" Kelley, a sportsman with more refined methods.

In pouncing upon their self-evident prey, Mr. Kelley was a shade the quicker. His elbow fended accurately the onslaught of Mr. McGuire.

"G'wan!" he commanded harshly. "I saw it first." McGuire *slunk* away, awed by superior intelligence. "Pardon me," said Mr. Kelley, to the General, "but you got balled up in the shuffle, didn't you? Let me assist you." He picked up the General's hat and brushed the dust from it.

The ways of Mr. Kelley could not but succeed. The General, bewildered and **dismayed** by the resounding streets, welcomed his deliverer as a *caballero* with a most disinterested heart. "I have a desire," said the General, "to return to the hotel of O'Brien, in which I am stop. Caramba! senor, there is a loudness and rapidness of going and coming in the city of this Nueva York."

Mr. Kelley's politeness would not suffer the distinguished Colombian to brave the dangers of the return unaccompanied. At the door of the Hotel Espanol they paused. A little lower down on the opposite side of the street shone the modest illuminated sign of El Refugio. Mr. Kelley, to whom few streets were unfamiliar, knew the place exteriorly as a "Dago joint." All foreigners, Mr. Kelley classed under the two heads of "Dagoes" and Frenchmen. He proposed to the General that they repair thither and *substantiate* their acquaintance with a liquid foundation.

An hour later found General Falcon and Mr. Kelley seated at a table in the conspirator's corner of El Refugio. Bottles and glasses were between them. For the tenth time the General confided the secret of his mission to the Estados Unidos. He

Fender - *A device on the front of a locomotive*
Slunk - *To move*
Caballero - *A spanish gentle man*
Substantiate - *Schemer*

was here, he declared, to purchase arms - 2,000 stands of Winchester rifles - for the Colombian revolutionists. He had drafts in his pocket drawn by the Cartagena Bank on its New York *correspondent* for $25,000. At other tables other revolutionists were shouting their political secrets to their fellow-plotters; but none was as loud as the General. He *pounded* the table; he hallooed for some wine; he roared to his friend that his *errand* was a secret one, and not to be hinted at to a living soul. Mr. Kelley himself was *stirred* to sympathetic *enthusiasm*. He grasped the General's hand across the table.

"Monseer," he said, *earnestly*, "I don't know where this country of yours is, but I'm for it. I guess it must be a branch of the United States, though, for the poetry guys and the school-marms call us Columbia, too, sometimes. It's a lucky thing for you that you butted into me to-night. I'm the only man in New York that can get this gun deal through for you. The Secretary of War of the United States is me best friend. He's in the city now, and I'll see him for you to-morrow. In the meantime, *monseer*, you keep them drafts tight in your inside pocket. I'll call for you to-morrow, and take you to see him. Say! that ain't the District of Columbia you're talking about, is it?" concluded Mr. Kelley, with a sudden *qualm*. "You can't capture that with no 2,000 guns - it's been tried with more."

"No, no, no!" exclaimed the General. "It is the Republic of Colombia - it is a g-r-reat republic on the top side of America of the South. Yes. Yes."

"All right," said Mr. Kelley, reassured. "Now suppose we trek along home and go by-by. I'll write to the Secretary to-night and make a date with him. It's a *ticklish* job to get guns out of New York. McClusky himself can't do it."

They parted at the door of the Hotel Espanol. The General rolled his eyes at the moon and sighed. "It is a great country, your Nueva York," he said. "Truly the cars in the streets devastate one, and the engine that cooks the nuts terribly makes a *squeak* in the ear. But, ah, Senor Kelley - the senoras with hair of much goldness, and admirable fatness - they are *magnificas*! Muy magnificas!"

Kelley went to the nearest telephone booth and called up McCrary's cafe, far up on Broadway. He asked for Jimmy Dunn.

"Is that Jimmy Dunn?" asked Kelley.

Errand - *A short and quick tip for a specific purpose*
Monieur - *A french title*
Qualm - *An uneasy feeling*
Ticklish - *Extremely sensitive*
Magnificas *-Magnificent*

"Yes," came the answer.

"You're a liar," sang back Kelley, joyfully. "Your'e the Secretary of War. Wait there till I come up. I've got the finest thing down here in the way of a fish you ever baited for. It's a Colorado-maduro, with a gold band around it and free coupons enough to buy a red hall lamp and a statuette of Psyche rubbering in the brook. I'll be up on the next car."

Jimmy Dunn was an A. M. of Crookdom. He was an artist in the confidence line. He never saw a bludgeon in his life; and he scorned knockout drops. In fact, he would have set nothing before an intended victim but the purest of drinks, if it had been possible to procure such a thing in New York. It was the ambition of "Spider" Kelley to elevate himself into Jimmy's class.

These two gentlemen held a conference that night at McCrary's. Kelley explained.

"He's as easy as a gumshoe. He's from the Island of Colombia, where there's a strike, or a feud, or something going on, and they've sent him up here to buy 2,000 Winchesters to **arbitrate** the thing with. He showed me two drafts for $10,000 each, and one for $5,000 on a bank here. 'S truth, Jimmy, I felt real mad with him because he didn't have it in thousand-dollar bills, and hand it to me on a silver waiter. Now, we've got to wait till he goes to the bank and gets the money for us."

They talked it over for two hours, and then Dunn said; "Bring him to No. __ Broadway, at four o'clock to-morrow afternoon."

In due time Kelley called at the Hotel Espanol for the General. He found the wily warrior engaged in **delectable** conversation with Mrs. O'Brien.

"The Secretary of War is waitin' for us," said Kelley.

The General tore himself away with an effort.

"Ay, **senor**," he said, with a sigh, "duty makes a call. But, senor, the senoras of your Estados Unidos - how beauties! For **exemplification**, take you la Madame O'Brien - que magnifica! She is one goddess - one Juno - what you call one ox-eyed Juno."

Now Mr. Kelley was a wit; and better men have been shrivelled by the fire of their own imagination. "Sure!" he said with a grin; "but you mean a peroxide Juno, don't you?"

Arbitrate - *To settle*
Delectable -
Delightful
Senor - *A spanish-speaking man*
Emplification - *An officially certifiedl copy of a document*

Mrs. O'Brien heard, and lifted an *auriferous* head. Her businesslike eye rested for an instant upon the disappearing form of Mr. Kelley. Except in street cars one should never be unnecessarily *rude* to a lady.

When the *gallant* Colombian and his escort arrived at the Broadway address, they were held in an anteroom for half an hour, and then admitted into a well-equipped office where a distinguished looking man, with a smooth face, wrote at a desk. General Falcon was presented to the Secretary of War of the United States, and his mission made known by his old friend, Mr. Kelley.

"Ah - Colombia!" said the Secretary, significantly, when he was made to understand; "I'm afraid there will be a little difficulty in that case. The President and I differ in our sympathies there. He prefers the established government, while I -" the secretary gave the General a mysterious but encouraging smile. "You, of course, know, General Falcon, that since the Tammany war, an act of Congress has been passed requiring all manufactured arms and *ammunition* exported from this country to pass through the War Department. Now, if I can do anything for you I will be glad to do so to oblige my old friend, Mr. Kelley. But it must be in absolute secrecy, as the President, as I have said, does not regard favourably the efforts of your revolutionary party in Colombia. I will have my orderly bring a list of the available arms now in the warehouse."

The Secretary struck a bell, and an orderly with the letters A. D. T. on his cap stepped promptly into the room.

"Bring me Schedule B of the small arms inventory," said the Secretary.

The orderly quickly returned with a printed paper. The Secretary studied it closely.

"I find," he said, "that in Warehouse 9, of Government stores, there is *shipment* of 2,000 stands of Winchester rifles that were ordered by the Sultan of Morocco, who forgot to send the cash with his order. Our rule is that legal-tender must be paid down at the time of purchase. My dear Kelley, your friend, General Falcon, shall have this lot of arms, if he desires it, at the manufacturer's price. And you will forgive me, I am sure, if I curtail our interview. I am expecting the Japanese Minister and Charles Murphy every moment!"

As one result of this interview, the General was deeply grateful to his *esteemed* friend, Mr. Kelley. As another, the

Shipment - *The act of sending of goods*
Auriferous - *Containing good*
Rude - *Crude, rough*
Gallant - *Smartly*

nimble Secretary of War was extremely busy during the next two days buying empty rifle cases and filling them with bricks, which were then stored in a *warehouse* rented for that purpose. As still another, when the General returned to the Hotel Espanol, Mrs. O'Brien went up to him, plucked a thread from his lapel, and said:

"Say, senor, I don't want to 'butt in,' but what does that monkey-faced, cat-eyed, rubber-necked tin horn tough want with you?"

"Sangre de mi vida!" exclaimed the General. "Impossible it is that you speak of my good friend, Senor Kelley."

"Come into the summer garden," said Mrs. O'Brien. "I want to have a talk with you."

Let us suppose that an hour has elapsed.

"And you say," said the General, "that for the sum of $18,000 can be purchased the *furnishment* of the house and the lease of one year with this garden so lovely - so *resembling* unto the *patios* of my cara Colombia?"

"And dirt cheap at that," sighed the lady.

"Ah, Dios!" breathed General Falcon. "What to me is war and politics? This spot is one *paradise*. My country it have other brave heroes to continue the fighting. What to me should be glory and the shooting of mans? Ah! no. It is here I have found one angel. Let us buy the Hotel Espanol and you shall be mine, and the money shall not be waste on guns." Mrs. O'Brien rested her blond pompadour against the shoulder of the Colombian *patriot*.

"Oh, senor," she sighed, happily, "ain't you terrible!"

Two days later was the time appointed for the delivery of the arms to the General. The boxes of supposed rifles were *stacked* in the rented warehouse, and the Secretary of War sat upon them, waiting for his friend Kelley to fetch the victim.

Mr. Kelley hurried, at the hour, to the Hotel Espanol. He found the General behind the desk adding up accounts.

"I have decide," said the General, "to buy not guns. I have to-day buy the insides of this hotel, and there shall be marrying of the General Perrico Ximenes Villablanca Falcon with la Madame O'Brien."

Mr. Kelley almost *strangled*.

Nimble - *Light/agile in movement*
Warehouse - *A place in which goods are stored*
Patios - *Roofless inner court yard*
Stacked - *Piled*

"Say, you old bald-headed bottle of shoe polish," he spluttered, "you're a *swindler* - that's what you are! You've bought a *boarding* house with money belonging to your *infernal* country, wherever it is."

"Ah," said the General, footing up a column, "that is what you call politics. War and revolution they are not nice. Yes. It is not best that one shall always follow Minerva. No. It is of quite desirable to keep hotels and be with that Juno - that ox-eyed Juno. Ah! what hair of the gold it is that she have!"

Mr. Kelley *choked* again.

"Ah, Senor Kelley!" said the General, feelingly and finally, "is it that you have never eaten of the corned *beef hash* that

Swindler - *To cheat*
Boarding - *Staying, residing*
Infernal - *Devilish*
Choked - *To stop the treath by squeezing*
Hash - *A dish of diced*

Madame O'Brien she make?"

Food For Thought

The author, O.Henry is famous for surprise endings and this story is no exception. However, the best part of the story is when the General suggest Kelley to eat the corned beef hash that his love, Madame O'Brien makes. Explain the expressions and feelings of Kelley at that spur of the moment in your own words.